U.S. Oil Imports and Exports

Neelesh Nerurkar
Specialist in Energy Policy

April 4, 2012

Congressional Research Service

7-5700

www.crs.gov

R42465

Summary

Over the last six years, net oil imports have fallen by 33% to average 8.4 million barrels per day (Mb/d) in 2011. This represents 45% of domestic consumption, down from 60% in 2005. Oil is a critical resource for the U.S. economy, but despite policy makers' longstanding concern, U.S. oil imports had generally increased for decades until peaking in 2005. Since then, the economic downturn and higher oil prices were a drag on oil consumption, while price-driven private investment and policy helped increase domestic supply of oil and oil alternatives. Net imports are gross imports minus exports. The decline in net imports has manifested itself as a decrease in gross imports and an increase in exports of petroleum products.

Gross U.S. imports of crude oil and petroleum products averaged 11.4 Mb/d in 2011, down 17% since 2005. More than a third of gross imports came from Canada and Mexico in 2011. About 40% came from members of the Organization for the Petroleum Exporting Countries (OPEC), mostly from OPEC members outside the Persian Gulf. Regionally, the largest share of U.S. imports come into the Gulf Coast region, which holds about half of U.S. refining capacity and sends petroleum products to other parts of the country and abroad. All regions of the country import more crude than refined products except for the East Coast, where petroleum products imports may rise further due to refinery closures.

U.S. oil exports, made up almost entirely of petroleum products, averaged 2.9 Mb/d in 2011. This is up from export of 1.2 Mb/d in 2005, led by growing export of distillates (diesel and related fuels) and gasoline. More than 60% of U.S. exports went to countries in the Western Hemisphere, particularly to countries such as Mexico and Canada from which the U.S. imports crude oil. Exports occur largely as a result of commercial decisions by oil market participants which reflect current oil market conditions as well as past investment in refining.

As a result, net oil imports fell from a peak of 12.5 Mb/d in 2005 to 8.4 Mb/d in 2011, their lowest level since 1995. A consensus is generally emerging among energy analysts that U.S. oil imports may be past their peak, reached in 2005. Imports as a share of consumption are expected to fall further, to less than 40% after 2020 driven by tighter fuel economy standards and increased domestic supply.

Despite the decline in net import volumes, the cost of net imports has increased due to rising oil prices. The aggregate national cost of oil imports is a function of the volume of oil imported and the price of that oil. The United States spent about $327 billion on net oil imports in 2011. Being a net importer of a particular good is not necessarily negative for an economy, but greater national oil import dependence can amplify the negative economic impacts of oil price increases.

Oil import and export developments pose a host of policy issues. Concerns about import dependence continue to generate interest in policy options to directly discourage imports or to reduce the need for imports by increasing domestic supply and decreasing demand. Rising exports at a time of rising prices has led to calls for policies to restrict such trade. The debate around the Keystone XL pipeline involves concerns about imports, exports, and the environment. The rising cost for fuels has led to calls for release of the Strategic Petroleum Reserve, meant to provide a short term policy option in case of supply disruptions. Policy options may entail various economic, fiscal, and environmental trade-offs.

Contents

Figures

Tables

Appendixes

Contacts

Introduction

Oil is a critical resource for the U.S. economy. It meets nearly 40% of total U.S. energy needs, including 94% of the energy used in transportation and 40% of the energy used by the industrial sector.[1] Unlike other forms of energy such as coal and natural gas, which are largely supplied from domestic sources, net imports from foreign sources meet 45% of U.S. oil consumption, and thus the basis of many of the nation's energy security concerns.

Figure 1. Net Oil Imports

In millions of barrels a day (Mb/d) and as share of U.S. consumption

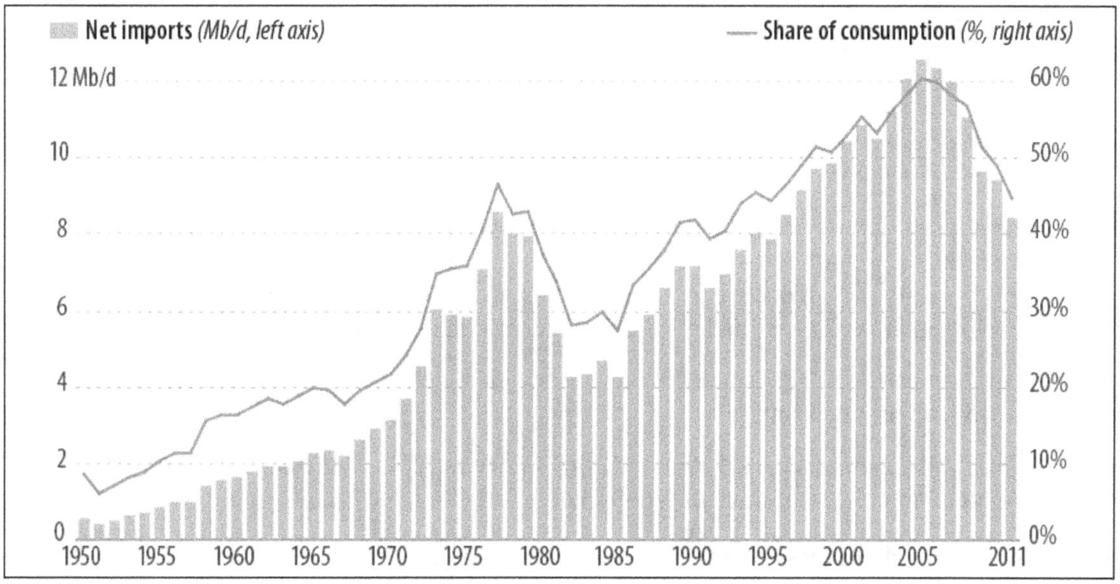

Data Source: EIA, *Petroleum & Other Liquid Fuels*, February 28, 2012, http://www.eia.gov/petroleum/data.cfm.

The United States has been concerned about dependence on foreign oil since it became a net oil importer in the late 1940s. Those concerns grew with import levels, especially in periods of high or rising oil prices. Nonetheless, imports have generally increased over the last six decades, except for a period following the oil spikes of the 1970s and again in the last six years. Net oil import volumes and share of consumption peaked in 2005 and then declined through 2011 as a result of economic and policy-driven changes in domestic supply and demand. See **Figure 1**. However, oil total (or aggregate) import costs have increased due to rising prices, which more than offset the savings from lower import volumes.

Net imports are gross imports minus exports (it is also the difference between domestic demand and supply). Interest in oil imports has climbed again as oil prices rebounded in response to

---

[1] U.S. Energy Information Administration, "Primary Energy Flow by Source and Sector, 2010," *Annual Energy Review 2010* (based on Tables 1.3, 2.1b-2.1f, 10.3, and 10.4), October 19, 2011, http://www.eia.gov/totalenergy/.

Unless otherwise mentioned, data in this report comes from the Energy Information Administration (EIA). Detailed import and export data from EIA may be found at http://www.eia.gov/petroleum/data.cfm#imports. Sources also include the *Short Term Energy Outlook* (http://www.eia.gov/forecasts/steo/), *Annual Energy Review* (http://www.eia.gov/totalenergy/data/annual/), and *Annual Energy Outlook* (http://www.eia.gov/forecasts/aeo/er/). All data accessed between February 27 and March 9.

---

global economic recovery in 2009-2010 and unrest in the Middle East and North Africa in 2011 (Libya, Egypt) and 2012 (tensions with Iran). Attention to oil exports grew in 2011, when the United States became a net exporter of petroleum products at a time when petroleum product prices were rising.[2] Though it remains a large net importer of oil due to the need for crude oil from abroad, the United States recently started exporting more petroleum products than it imports.

The U.S. oil supply-demand balance is presented for context in **Table 1**. It shows U.S. oil consumption and production as well as the resulting net imports, gross imports, and exports:

- In 2011, the United States consumed 18.8 million barrels a day (Mb/d) of petroleum products, down 2 Mb/d or 9% since 2005. The decline was widespread among petroleum products, including gasoline, distillates (includes diesel and heating oil), and jet fuel.

- Domestic production of oil and related liquid fuels was 9.2 Mb/d in 2011, up 1.8 Mb/d or 24% since 2005. The increase was led by higher production of onshore crude oil in the lower 48 states, fuel ethanol, and natural gas liquids.

- As a result of lower consumption and higher production, the need for imported oil fell. Net imports fell from 60% of domestic consumption in 2005 to 45% in 2011. The 4.1 Mb/d decline in net imports over in six years reflected a 2.4 Mb/d decline in gross imports and a 1.8 Mb/d increase in exports.

- Gross imports fell 17% since 2005, including declines in both crude oil and petroleum products imports.

- Gross oil exports increased by about 150% since 2005. U.S. gross exports were equal to about 15% of the U.S. oil market in 2011.

This report first explains these oil import and export volumes, including sources and destinations of traded oil. It then turns to the value of oil trade in the total U.S. trade balance for goods and services. Finally, several key policy issues regarding imports are discussed.

---

[2] Petroleum products are obtained from the processing of crude oil (including lease condensate), natural gas, and other hydrocarbon compounds. Petroleum products include unfinished oils, liquefied petroleum gases, pentanes plus, aviation gasoline, motor gasoline, naphtha-type jet fuel, kerosene-type jet fuel, kerosene, distillate fuel oil, residual fuel oil, petrochemical feedstocks, special naphthas, lubricants, waxes, petroleum coke, asphalt, road oil, still gas, and miscellaneous products (http://www.eia.gov/tools/glossary/index.cfm?id=P).

Table 1. U.S. Supply-Demand Balance

In million barrels a day (Mb/d), numbers in parenthesis indicate negative values

	2000	2005	2010	2011	*Change 2005-2011*
Consumption	**19.7**	**20.8**	**19.2**	**18.8**	*(2.0)*
Gasoline	8.5	9.2	9.0	8.7	*(0.4)*
Distillates (inc. Diesel, Heating oil)	3.7	4.1	3.8	3.9	*(0.3)*
Jet Fuel	1.7	1.7	1.4	1.4	*(0.3)*
Propane and Heavier Liquefied Petroleum Gas	1.5	1.4	1.3	1.2	*(0.1)*
Other Petroleum Consumption	4.3	4.5	3.7	3.6	*(0.9)*
Domestic Production	**8.3**	**7.4**	**8.7**	**9.2**	*1.8*
Domestic Crude Oil Production	5.8	5.2	5.5	5.6	*0.4*
Onshore Lower 48	3.4	3.0	3.3	3.7	*0.7*
Alaska	1.0	0.9	0.6	0.6	*(0.3)*
Federal Gulf of Mexico	1.4	1.3	1.6	1.3	*0.0*
Natural Gas Liquids	1.9	1.7	2.1	2.2	*0.5*
Fuel Ethanol	0.1	0.3	0.9	0.9	*0.7*
Other Domestic Production	0.4	0.3	0.3	0.5	*0.2*
Other Supply	**1.0**	**0.8**	**1.0**	**1.2**	**0.4**
Refinery Processing Gains	1.0	1.0	1.1	1.1	*0.1*
Change in Inventories	0.1	(0.1)	(0.0)	0.1	*0.3*
Net Imports	**10.4**	**12.6**	**9.4**	**8.5**	*(4.1)*
Crude Oil	9.0	10.1	9.2	8.9	*(1.2)*
Petroleum Products	1.4	2.5	0.3	(0.4)	*(2.9)*
Gasoline	0.3	1.0	0.5	0.3	*(0.7)*
Distillates (inc. Diesel, Heating oil)	0.1	0.2	(0.4)	(0.7)	*(0.9)*
Other Products	1.0	1.3	0.2	(0.0)	*(1.4)*
Gross Exports	*1.0*	*1.2*	*2.4*	*2.9*	*1.8*
Gross Imports	*11.5*	*13.7*	*11.8*	*11.4*	*(2.4)*
Net Imports as a Share of Consumption	*53%*	*60%*	*49%*	*45%*	*-15%*

Data Sources: EIA, *Short-Term Energy Outlook* (http://www.eia.gov/forecasts/steo/) and *Petroleum & Other Liquid Fuels* (http://www.eia.gov/petroleum/data.cfm).

Notes: Onshore Lower 48 also includes state offshore production. Natural Gas Liquids includes ethane, propane, butane, and other lighter hydrocarbons. Other Domestic Production includes non-ethanol oxygenates and EIA adjustments. Refinery Processing Gains are the volumetric increases that take place when refining a barrel of crude oil into petroleum products; these gains are based on refining both domestic and imported crude. Inventories can also be of domestic or foreign origin. A positive change in inventories indicates more was withdrawn from inventories than put in over the course of the year. Individual items may not sum to the total due to rounding.

U.S. Oil Imports and Exports

The United States both imports and exports oil. It imports both crude oil and petroleum products. Oil exports are almost entirely in the form of petroleum products as a result of economic and policy factors.

Gross Imports

The United States imported 11.4 Mb/d of oil in 2011. This included 8.9 Mb/d of crude oil and 2.4 Mb/d of petroleum products (see **Table 2**). Gross imports peaked in 2005 and have fallen five of the following six years. The decline was split between crude oil and petroleum products. Gross imports are at their lowest level since 2002.

Table 2. Gross Imports by Fuel

In Mb/d

Fuel	2000	2005	2010	2011	Change 2005-2011
Total	**11.5**	**13.7**	**11.8**	**11.4**	**(2.4)**
Crude Oil	9.1	10.1	9.2	8.9	(1.2)
Petroleum Products	2.4	3.6	2.6	2.4	(1.1)
Natural Gas Liquids	0.3	0.4	0.2	0.2	(0.2)
Gasoline	0.7	1.1	0.9	0.8	(0.3)
Distillates (inc. Diesel, Heating oil)	0.3	0.3	0.2	0.2	(0.2)
Residual Fuel Oil	0.4	0.5	0.4	0.4	(0.2)
Petroleum Coke	0.0	0.0	0.0	0.0	(0.0)
Other	0.8	1.2	0.9	0.9	(0.3)

Source: EIA, *Petroleum & Other Liquid Fuels*, February 28, 2012, http://www.eia.gov/petroleum/data.cfm.

Notes: Gasoline includes finished motor gasoline and motor gasoline blending components, but does not include biofuels. Other includes petrochemical feedstocks, biofuels, unfinished oils, and other petroleum products.

Imports by Source

More than a third of U.S. gross imports came from Canada and Mexico in 2011. About 40% came from members of the Organization of the Petroleum Exporting Countries (OPEC), though most of this is from OPEC countries outside the Persian Gulf, such as Venezuela, Nigeria, Algeria, and Angola. (See **Figure 2**.) Imports from OPEC countries are nearly all crude oil. Imports from Non-OPEC countries are also mostly crude oil, though the United States does import some petroleum products from Canada, Europe, and Asia.

Oil trading patterns can shift due to market conditions, but much of the oil that companies import to the United States comes from the same countries month to month. While many kinds of crude oil are interchangeable to some degree—which reinforces the globally integrated nature of the oil market—each has unique characteristics. Refineries optimize their operations for particular grades of crude oil.[3] Proximity, infrastructure, and trading relationships may also contribute to normal trade patterns and determine which crude oils are consumed in certain countries.

Over the last several years, imports of oil from many countries fell with the general trend of falling imports. The decline in imports from some specific countries was exacerbated by their declining output. For example, declining oil output from Mexico, the United Kingdom, and Norway contributed to lower imports from those countries.[4] Imports from OPEC can fall at times when OPEC curtails its output in its efforts to manage the oil market and oil prices as it did to stem falling oil prices in late 2008/early 2009.[5] Despite the general downward trend in imports since 2005, imports from some countries did rise, including Canada, Colombia, and Brazil. Canadian imports rose from 2.1 Mb/d in 2005 to 2.7 Mb/d in 2011. The share of gross imports from Canada increased from 16% to 24%.

> ### Decisions in the U.S. Oil Market
>
> Unlike some nations around the world in which oil production, refining, trade, and marketing are dominated by government-owned national oil companies, these functions are carried out by numerous privately owned companies in the United States. The size and characteristics of U.S. oil trade and its variation over time result from myriad decisions by a multitude of individual U.S. oil companies in response to domestic and global market opportunities and demands. Although these companies operate under U.S. state and federal policies, and their decisions are affected by these policies, there is no centralized control and direction of oil imports and exports in the United States.

Figure 2. Gross Imports by Major Sources

Share of gross oil imports, 2011

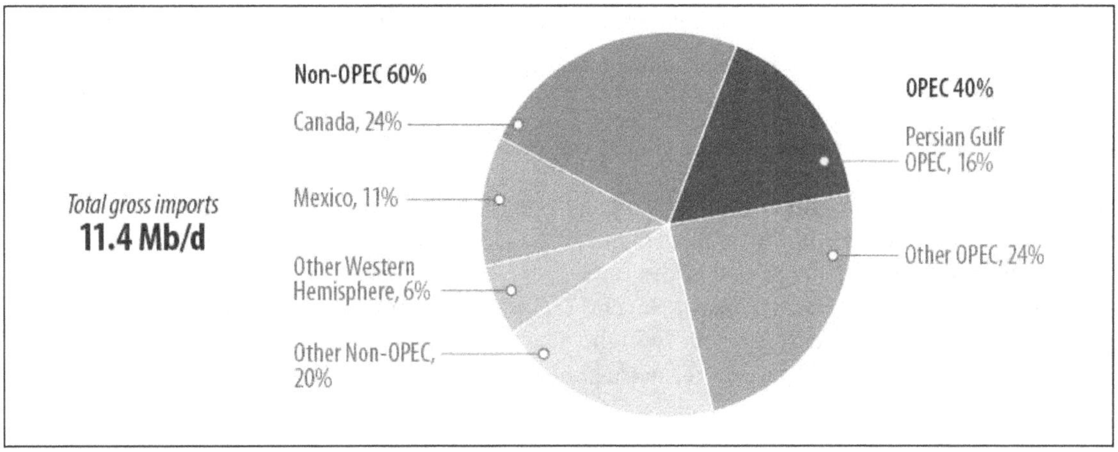

Data Source: EIA, *Petroleum & Other Liquid Fuels*, February 28, 2012, http://www.eia.gov/petroleum/data.cfm.

Notes: "Persian Gulf OPEC" members are Saudi Arabia, Kuwait, United Arab Emirates, Iraq, and Qatar (the United States does not import oil from Iran). "Other OPEC" members are Angola, Nigeria, Algeria, Libya, Venezuela, and Ecuador.

---

[3] For more on refining, see CRS Report R41478, *The U.S. Oil Refining Industry: Background in Changing Markets and Fuel Policies*, by Anthony Andrews, Robert Pirog, and Molly F. Sherlock.

[4] Mexican output fell sharply due to depletion at the giant Cantarell field. Efforts to offset the decline from other sources have been hampered by difficulties at the Mexican national oil company, Pemex, and restrictions on foreign investment.

[5] For details on how OPEC manages oil supply, see CRS Report R42024, *Oil Price Fluctuations*, by Neelesh Nerurkar and Mark Jickling.

Imports by U.S. Region

Regionally, the largest share of U.S. imports come into the Gulf Coast region, which also has about half of the refining capacity in the United States. (See **Table 3**, exports discussed in the next section). Much of that crude oil brought into the Gulf Coast is refined and sent to other parts of the country via pipeline. The Gulf Coast receives imports from around the world, and around 90% of these imports are in the form of crude oil.

Table 3. 2011 Oil Imports and Exports by Region

In Mb/d

Region	Imports			Exports		
	Total	Crude Oil	Petroleum Products	Total	Crude Oil	Petroleum Products
Total	11.4	8.9	2.4	2.9	0.0	2.9
East Coast (PADD1)	2.3	1.0	1.3	0.3	0.0	0.3
Midwest (PADD2)	1.6	1.5	0.1	0.1	0.0	0.1
Gulf Coast (PADD3)	5.8	4.9	0.9	2.2	0.0	2.2
Rockies (PADD4)	0.3	0.3	0.0	0.0	0.0	0.0
West Coast (PADD5)	1.3	1.2	0.2	0.3	0.0	0.3

Source: EIA, *Petroleum & Other Liquid Fuels,* February 28, 2012, http://www.eia.gov/petroleum/data.cfm.

Notes: The United States is divided into five Petroleum Administration for Defense Districts (PADDs). These were created during World War II under the Petroleum Administration for War to help organize the allocation of fuels derived from petroleum products, including gasoline and diesel (or "distillate") fuel. Today, these regions are still used for data collection purposes. PADD5 includes Hawaii and Alaska.

All regions of the country import more crude than petroleum products except for the East Coast, which received petroleum products from Canada, St. Croix, Russia, Europe, and elsewhere in 2011. Petroleum products imports into the East Coast are set to grow due to the closure of refining capacity in the U.S. Northeast. Several factors will complicate substitute sources of supply reaching the Northeast, especially in the near term, including constraints on import infrastructure and closure of several refineries in Europe and the Caribbean, traditionally sources of North East imports.

More than half of the petroleum products imported into the East Coast are gasoline and diesel. Export of these products from the Gulf Coast has been growing. There are several barriers to bringing more of these products from the Gulf Coast to the East Coast rather than sending them abroad. First, pipeline capacity from the Gulf Coast to the Northeast is at or near capacity. There are plans to expand this capacity in the future. Second, seaborne movements are constrained in part by the Jones Act: Section 27 of the Merchant Marine Act of 1920 (P.L. 66-261) which requires trade between U.S. ports to be carried on U.S. flagged vessels built in the United States, owned by U.S. citizens, and crewed by U.S. crews. According to reports, the existing Jones Act tanker fleet is fully employed in existing oil trade between U.S. ports and little or no tanker capacity is available for additional shipments from Gulf Cost to the Northeast.[6] The American

---

[6] Energy Information Administration, *Potential Impacts of Reductions in Refinery Activity on Northeast Petroleum Product Markets,* February 27, 2012, http://www.eia.gov/analysis/petroleum/nerefining/update/.

Maritime Partnership, the trade association for Jones Act shippers, has responded that there is available barge capacity to carry additional petroleum products. According to an EIA report:

> Consider a trip from Houston to Philadelphia. A 325,000-barrel tanker has economies of scale that make it more economic than the smaller barge movements that typically move on this route. While terms may vary with specific circumstances, such a tanker might cost around 7 cents per gallon for a round trip. Articulated Tug Barges (ATBs) would be less efficient than tankers, but more efficient than a towed barge. A barge cost for this route might run around 15 cents per gallon, perhaps a little less for the ATBs and a little more for towed barges. Tankers are in high demand and are usually booked well ahead of time. ATBs and large barges would likely be used for some of the movements to the Northeast, at least initially.
>
> With transportation rates around 15 cents per gallon reportedly for Gulf Coast-Northeast barge movements, imports may be more economic for some of the needed volumes of Ultra low sulfur diesel (USLD). Foreign tankers are available, and a tanker moving product from Europe to New York Harbor (3,400 nautical miles) cost around 5-9 cents per gallon this past year, similar to the tanker costs from the Gulf Coast to New York Harbor.[7]

According to a U.S. shipping industry source, existing tankers currently engaged in relatively shorter routes, such as between Texas and Florida, could be diverted to routes between the Gulf Coast and the North East; the shorter routes may be taken up by available barge vessels.[8] The price impacts of such a scenario are not clear. Separately, there are also infrastructure constraints on shifting from petroleum products supplied by regional refineries to seaborne and new pipeline sources. Issues involved in supplying petroleum products to the Northeast market are covered in detail in the EIA report *Potential Impacts of Reductions in Refinery Activity on Northeast Petroleum Product Markets.*[9]

Oil Exports

Almost all U.S. exports are petroleum products, not crude oil, due to both policy (discussed below in "Export Restrictions on Crude Oil and Petroleum Products") and commercial factors, particularly that the U.S. needs more crude than it produces.[10] Market conditions—the needs (and ability to pay) of specific buyers and sellers in different parts of the world at a given time—can drive the export of some petroleum product cargos even when the United States generally imports oil. In recent years, moderating demand at home, the resulting available refining capacity, and rising demand abroad has led to rising U.S. exports of diesel and gasoline. Exports have increased from 1.2 Mb/d in 2005 to 2.9 Mb/d in 2011. The largest share of the increase has been in distillate fuels, which includes diesel and heating oil. (See **Table 4**.) Export of gasoline has also increased.

---

[7] Energy Information Administration, *Adding Barges to EIA Study Still Leaves Concerns*, This Week In Petroleum, April 4, 2012, http://www.eia.gov/oog/info/twip/twip.asp.

[8] "Oceangoing barges could meet gap in US Northeast gasoline, ULSD supply," *Platts*, March 23, 2012.

[9] See footnote 7.

[10] The United States exports a small amount of crude oil to Canada, about 50 Kb/d in 2011.

Table 4. Oil Exports by Fuel

In Mb/d

Fuel	2000	2005	2010	2011	Change 2005-2011
Total	**1.0**	**1.2**	**2.4**	**2.9**	**1.8**
Crude Oil	0.1	0.0	0.0	0.0	0.0
Petroleum Products	1.0	1.1	2.3	2.9	1.7
Natural Gas Liquids	0.1	0.1	0.2	0.2	0.1
Gasoline	0.2	0.2	0.3	0.5	0.4
Distillates (inc. Diesel, Heating oil)	0.2	0.1	0.7	0.9	0.7
Residual Fuel Oil	0.1	0.3	0.4	0.4	0.2
Petroleum Coke	0.3	0.3	0.4	0.5	0.1
Other	0.1	0.2	0.3	0.4	0.2

Source: EIA, *Petroleum & Other Liquid Fuels*, February 28, 2012, http://www.eia.gov/petroleum/data.cfm.

Notes: See Notes for Table 2.

In 2011, more than 60% of U.S. exports went to countries in the Western Hemisphere. The largest recipients were Mexico, Canada, and Brazil. The United States is a net oil importer from all three—they send more crude oil to the United States than they receive in refined products from the United States. Of the 0.5 Mb/d of total gasoline exports, nearly 60% go to Mexico.[11] Exports of other fuels are more diversified. See **Table 5** for a list of major destinations for all oil exports.

Table 5. Exports by Destination

In Mb/d

Destination	2011 Exports
Total	2.9
Canada	0.3
Mexico	0.6
Brazil	0.2
Other Western Hemisphere	0.8
European Union	0.3
Other	0.8

Source: EIA, *Petroleum & Other Liquid Fuels*, February 28, 2012, http://www.eia.gov/petroleum/data.cfm.

---

[11] For instance, some of the crude oil supply from Mexico is purchased by the Deer Park Refinery in Texas, which Petroleos Mexicanos (PEMEX), Mexico's national oil company, co-owns with Shell. According to reports, PEMEX sends its share of the refinery's gasoline output back to Mexico. PEMEX is considering acquiring additional refining assets in the United States to meet gasoline demand in Mexico. (Carlos Manuel Rodriguez, "Pemex Seeks to Buy 'Significant' U.S. Refining Asset This Year, CEO Says," Bloomberg, March 9, 2011.)

Why Does the United States Export Oil?

Exports occur as a result of commercial decisions by oil market participants which reflect current oil market conditions as well as past investment in refining. Export of crude oil is prohibited except in several specific cases, but there are almost no limits on export of refined product. Traditionally, most U.S. oil exports had been mostly heavier petroleum products, such as residual fuel oil or petroleum coke, for which there is limited demand in the United States, or products that do not meet U.S environmental standards.[12] However, as shown in **Table 4**, the growth in exports in recent years has been led by diesel and gasoline. At 2.9 Mb/d, total oil exports are equivalent to about 15% of the almost 19 Mb/d U.S. domestic oil market.

The growth in exports of gasoline and diesel reflect shifting market conditions. U.S. oil needs declined due to the recession, high prices, greater fuel economy,[13] and growth of ethanol.[14] Meanwhile, rapid economic growth in emerging markets such as China has led to a robust increase in oil demand. Much of that demand growth in recent years has been concentrated in distillates such as diesel.[15] Gasoline demand has also been relatively stronger in emerging markets, versus flat to falling demand in advanced economies such as the United States or Europe. However, advanced economies have been the traditional centers of demand in the global oil market. Industry has built refineries in those countries over decades to meet that demand. With demand at home weak and refining capacity already built, some refiners have looked to markets abroad. Rising exports at a time of rising prices for gasoline, diesel, and other refined products has prompted calls by some to ban export of refined products. This is discussed below in "Export Restrictions on Crude Oil and Petroleum Products."

Net Imports Fall by 33% Since 2005

Net oil imports—gross imports minus exports—fell from a peak of 12.5 Mb/d in 2005 to 8.4 Mb/d in 2011. Underlying this shift is a decline in crude oil imports and the shift from being a net petroleum products importer to an exporter. Net import volumes are at their lowest level since 1995.

Crude oil imports were 8.9 Mb/d and exports were less than 0.1 Mb/d. Petroleum products imports were 2.4 Mb/d and exports were 2.9 Mb/d. Due to its large crude oil imports, the United States remained a large net importer of oil. See **Table 6**. The United States is the world's largest oil importer, followed by China, whose net oil imports were about two-thirds that of the United States in 2011.[16]

---

[12] CRS Report R40120, *U.S. Oil Exports*, by Robert Bamberger.

[13] National Highway Traffic Safety Administration, U.S. Department of Transportation, *Summary of Fuel Economy Standards*, October 28, 2011, http://www.nhtsa.gov/staticfiles/rulemaking/pdf/cafe/October_2011_Public.pdf.

[14] Retail gasoline is now a blend of 10% ethanol in most parts of the country. This reduces how much unblended gasoline, a product of refineries, is needed. Ethanol is usually blended at petroleum product distribution centers before the product is sent to retail stations.

[15] *BP Statistical Review of World Energy 2011*, BP Plc., June 2011, http://www.bp.com/statisticalreview.

[16] China imported 6.2 Mb/d of crude oil and refined products (primarily crude oil) and exported about 0.6 Mb/d (primarily refined products, though it is a net refined products importer). China's General Customs Administration data provided by Hong Kong Trade Development Council, http://www.hktdc.com/info/mi/ccs/en/China-Statistics.htm. Conversion factors from the BP Statistical Review of World Energy, http://www.bp.com/statisticalreview. Accessed March 8, 2012.

Table 6. Petroleum Trade Balance by Liquid Fuel Type

In Mb/d, negative values are in parentheses and indicate gross or net imports (in net columns)

	Net			2011		
	2000	**2005**	**2010**	**Imports**	**Exports**	**Net**
Total	(10.4)	(12.5)	(9.4)	(11.4)	2.9	(8.4)
Crude Oil	(9.0)	(10.1)	(9.2)	(8.9)	0.0	(8.9)
Petroleum Products	(1.4)	(2.5)	(0.3)	(2.4)	2.9	0.4
Natural Gas Liquids	(0.1)	(0.3)	(0.0)	(0.2)	0.2	0.0
Gasoline	(0.3)	(1.0)	(0.5)	(0.8)	0.5	(0.3)
Distillates (inc. Diesel, Heating oil)	(0.1)	(0.2)	0.4	(0.2)	0.9	0.7
Residual Fuel Oil	(0.2)	(0.3)	0.0	(0.4)	0.4	0.1
Petroleum Coke	0.3	0.3	0.4	(0.0)	0.5	0.5
Other	(1.0)	(1.0)	(0.6)	(0.9)	0.4	(0.5)

Source: EIA, *Petroleum & Other Liquid Fuels*, February 28, 2012, http://www.eia.gov/petroleum/data.cfm.

Notes: 2000-2010 figures are exports minus imports. Parentheses indicate a negative balance (more imports than exports). 2011 figures show imports, exports, and balance. "Other unfinished" includes non-crude unfinished liquid fuels. Gasoline includes finished motor gasoline and gasoline blending components.

Because some U.S. exports of petroleum products go to some of the countries from which the United States imports crude oil, such as Mexico and Brazil, the sources of net imports look different than the sources of gross imports. The United States export few petroleum products to OPEC members, so their share of net imports is larger than their share of gross imports. (See **Figure 3**; compare to **Figure 2**).

Figure 3. Net Imports by Major Sources

Share of net oil imports, 2011

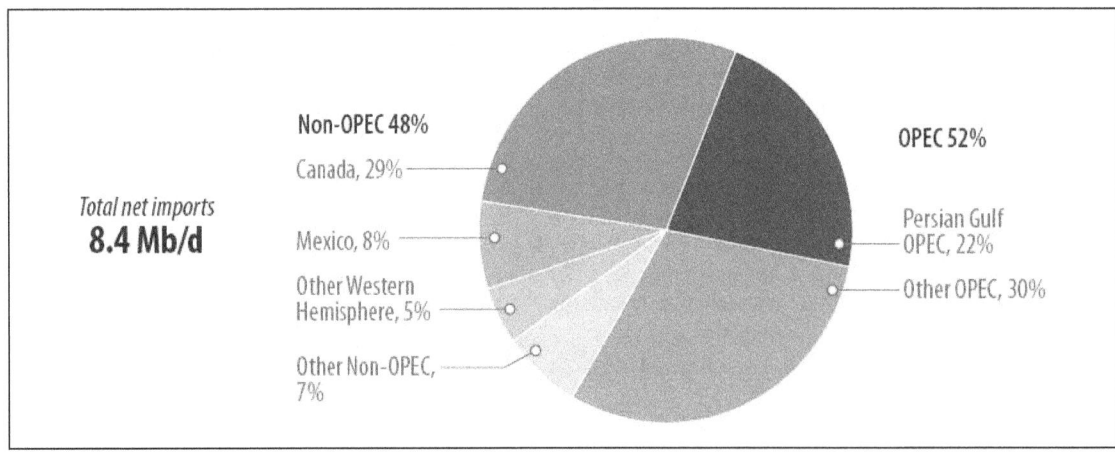

Data Source: EIA, *Petroleum & Other Liquid Fuels*, February 28, 2012, http://www.eia.gov/petroleum/data.cfm.

Notes: "Persian Gulf OPEC" members are Saudi Arabia, Kuwait, United Arab Emirates, Iraq and Qatar (the United States does not import oil from Iran). "Other OPEC" members are Angola, Nigeria, Algeria, Libya, Venezuela, and Ecuador.

Looking Forward: Falling Oil Import Dependence

A consensus is emerging among energy analysts that U.S. oil imports may be past their peak, reached in 2005. Further, some expect that imports may fall both in terms of absolute volumes and as a share of U.S. consumption. The EIA projects that net oil imports, already down by 4.1 Mb/d since 2005, will fall by an additional 1 Mb/d by 2020, leveling out at near 7.5 Mb/d through 2035 in its long-term forecast reference case. (See **Figure 4**.) This forecast would correspond to net oil imports declining from 60% of domestic consumption in 2005 to 45% in 2011 and to less than 40% after 2020.

Market analysts have reached the conclusion that import dependence will decline as the forces that pushed imports down in recent years become evident. While some of these recent forces are temporary—for example, those related specifically to the recession—some are expected to persist: high oil prices, rising efficiency, and greater domestic production of crude oil, natural gas liquids, and alternative fuels. The evolution over time of EIA import projections is illustrated in **Figure 4**. However, even with import volumes flat, import costs may still rise if oil prices increase.

Figure 4. Lower Expectations for Future Oil Imports

In Mb/d

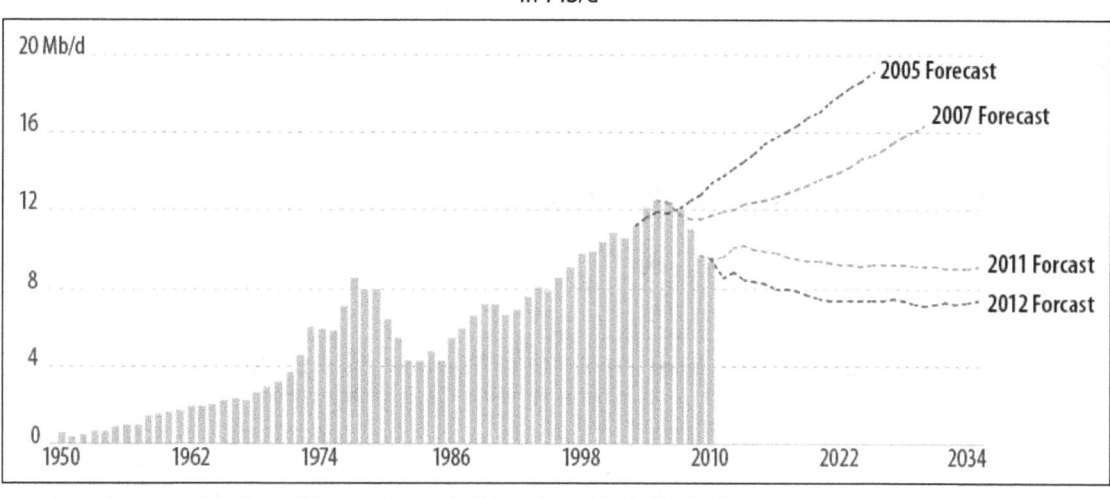

Data Source: EIA, Annual Energy Outlook (AEO) from 2005, 2007, 2011, and the preliminary 2012 AEO. For each year, forecasts are EIA's "Reference Case" projection. http://www.eia.doe.gov/forecasts/aeo/index.cfm. Also, EIA Annual Energy Review, http://www.eia.gov/totalenergy/data/annual/.

Oil, the Trade Balance, and U.S. Economy

Despite the decline in net import volumes, the cost of net imports has generally increased due to rising oil prices. The aggregate national cost of oil imports is a function of the volume of oil imported and exported and the price of that oil. The United States spent about $327 billion on net oil imports in 2011 (see **Table 7**). Despite lower import volumes, the cost has increased from the $229 billion spent in 2005,[17] as well as amounts spent in 2009 and 2010 shown below. While

---

[17] *U.S. International Trade in Goods and Services – Annual Revisions for 2005 (FT900)*, U.S. Census Bureau and U.S. (continued...)

fewer barrels were imported on a net (and gross) basis in 2011, each of those barrels cost more. The price increase more than offset the volume decrease with respect to total costs.

The cost of net imports in 2011 was lower than the record high of $386 billion reached in 2008. While the per barrel cost of crude was 8% higher in 2011 than in 2008, net imports had declined by 24%.[18] (In nominal terms, 2011 had the highest average annual oil prices ever, and the second highest price ever in inflation adjusted terms). Lower import volumes and higher export volumes contributed to keeping the net costs lower.

Table 7. Energy Trade in the U.S. Trade Balance

In billions of U.S. dollars

	Imports			Exports			Trade Balance		
	2009	2010	2011	2009	2010	2011	2009	2010	2011
Total Oil	254	336	439	49	71	113	(205)	(265)	(327)
Crude Oil	189	252	332	1	1	2	(188)	(251)	(330)
Other Oil	65	84	108	48	70	111	(17)	(14)	3
Natural Gas	16	17	15	3	5	6	(13)	(12)	(9)
Electricity	2	2	2	1	1	0	(2)	(1)	(2)
Nuclear fuel	5	6	6	2	2	3	(3)	(4)	(3)
Coal	2	2	3	7	10	17	4	8	14
Total Energy	279	363	465	62	89	139	(218)	(275)	(326)
Total Goods and Services	1,956	2,338	2,661	1,575	1,838	2,103	(381)	(500)	(558)
Energy Share	14%	16%	17%	4%	5%	7%	57%	55%	58%
Oil Share	13%	14%	17%	3%	4%	5%	54%	53%	59%

Source: *U.S. International Trade in Goods and Services (FT900)*, reports for December 2011 (February 12, 2012) and 2010 Annual Revisions (June 9, 2011), U.S. Census Bureau and U.S. Bureau of Economic Analysis, http://www.census.gov/foreign-trade/data/index.html.

Notes: Other oil includes Petroleum Products, other; Fuel oil; natural gas liquids (for import data), and liquefied petroleum gases (for export data). Coal includes Coal and related fuels and metallurgical grade coal (for export data).

These considerations prompt two questions: how oil import costs can affect the economy and why oil prices rose despite the decline in U.S. consumption and the rise in production.

(...continued)

Bureau of Economic Analysis, June 9, 2006, http://www.census.gov/foreign-trade/data/index.html. Includes crude oil, fuel oil, petroleum products, liquefied petroleum gases, and natural gas liquids.

[18] Refiners acquisition cost of crude averaged $94.74 per barrel in 2008 and $101.92 per barrel in 2011.

How Do Oil Imports Affect the Economy?

Being a net importer of a particular good is not necessarily negative for an economy: The United States imports many products because they would be more costly to consumers, businesses, or taxpayers were they produced domestically. But import dependence for an item can have negative economic impacts, particularly if it contributes to long-term trade deficits or when prices for that good increase. Trade deficits are ultimately financed by borrowing from abroad, which generates financial obligations for future repayment. Positive and negative impacts of trade deficits are explained in CRS Report RL31032, *The U.S. Trade Deficit: Causes, Consequences, and Policy Options*, by Craig K. Elwell.

Greater national oil import dependence can also amplify the negative economic impacts of oil price increases. An increase in the price of crude oil can quickly translate to higher prices for petroleum products like gasoline. Rising oil product prices strain the budgets of households and businesses, reducing their savings and/or spending on other goods and services, some of which would have been produced domestically. Gasoline prices, in particular, are one of the most visible consumer prices, which may amplify their influence on consumers. For imported oil, that wealth is sent abroad, and only a portion of it is returned via now wealthier oil exporting countries buying more U.S. products.

Even with oil from domestic sources, an oil price increase redistributes wealth within the economy from oil consumers to domestic oil producers, which may cause economic dislocation as businesses and workers adjust to the change. The impact can be exacerbated when the price change is faster as it makes the dislocations more abrupt. Economic analysts estimate that the impact of a sustained $10 per barrel increase in the price of oil could result in about 0.2% lower economic growth and 120,000 fewer jobs in the first year after the increase.[19] Rapidly rising oil prices likely contributed to the U.S. economic recession in 2007-2008.[20]

If the United States were not a net importer of oil—if it produced as much oil as it consumed— rising oil prices would not increase the import bill, but would still negatively impact the budgets of many U.S. households and businesses. Wealth would be redistributed from oil consumers to oil producers within the economy. Oil prices paid by U.S. consumers for petroleum products would still be affected by international events as long as oil trade was permitted. Other impacts of higher oil prices, like inflation and unemployment, may continue to be economic concerns.

The relationship between oil prices, oil imports, and the U.S. economy are discussed in greater detail in CRS Report R42024, *Oil Price Fluctuations*, by Neelesh Nerurkar and Mark Jickling.

---

[19] Nigel Gault, "Oil Prices and the U.S. Economy: Some Rules of Thumb," *IHS Global Insight Inc.*, February 24, 2011. Estimates from other forecasters of the Gross Domestic Product (GDP) impact of a $10 per barrel increase are similar, including those from the Federal Reserve according to reports (Robin Harding, "Oil Surge Puts Fragile US Recovery at Risk," *Financial Times*, February 24, 2011).

[20] James Hamilton, *Causes and Consequences of the Oil Shock of 2007-08*, Brookings Institute, Brookings Papers on Economic Activity, March 23, 2009, p. 40, http://www.brookings.edu/economics/bpea/~/media/Files/Programs/ES/BPEA/2009_spring_bpea_papers/2009_spring_bpea_hamilton.pdf.

Why Are Oil Prices Rising?

Rising oil prices have increased oil import costs despite falling oil import volumes. The increase in oil prices can be difficult to understand if looking only at the United States. As described above, U.S domestic production has increased and U.S. consumption has fallen (See **Table 1**). Understanding these changes requires looking at the global oil market.

The oil market—both for crude oil and petroleum products—is globally integrated. More than 60% of global oil supply is traded internationally. Global oil prices tend to move together and developments anywhere in the oil market can affect oil prices everywhere. Despite developments in the United States, global oil consumption is at an all time high. It is expected to continue growing for the foreseeable future, led by demand from emerging market countries. In light of this demand growth, there are concerns about the adequacy of global supply.

These concerns about supply and demand are borne out of recent experience. See **Figure 5**. Oil prices have generally increased since 2002. Rapid, energy-intensive economic growth in emerging market countries has meant they have been leading global oil demand growth. Global oil supply was unable to keep up with demand at previously prevailing prices. Depletion of some easy-to-produce resources, the oil industry's difficult shift to more complex resources, geopolitical and weather-related supply disruptions, and restrictions on oil production in resource rich countries all hampered supply growth. Oil prices rose to balance the market, pricing out some consumers and incentivizing additional supply. Prices collapsed with the global economic downturn in 2008, but the respite was temporary. Prices recovered as economic growth returned, particularly in emerging markets, and new geopolitical developments again raised concerns about global supply.

The unrest in Egypt, Libya, and other parts of the Middle East and North Africa contributed to higher oil prices in 2011, as have tensions with Iran in 2012. Supply disruptions or risk of supply disruptions to particular sources of oil production (and transportation) can raise oil costs even to countries that do not import oil from these sources. The United States imported little oil from Libya prior to unrest there in 2011 and imports no oil from Iran, though disruptions or risk of disruptions related to those countries contributed to higher oil prices in the United States. Those who do purchase oil from these sources have to find alternative sources when their supply is disrupted. These customers can bid up the cost of oil from elsewhere, contributing to higher global oil prices.

Figure 5. Oil Price and Selected Global Oil Market Events

Price for West Texas Intermediate Crude Oil (WTI)

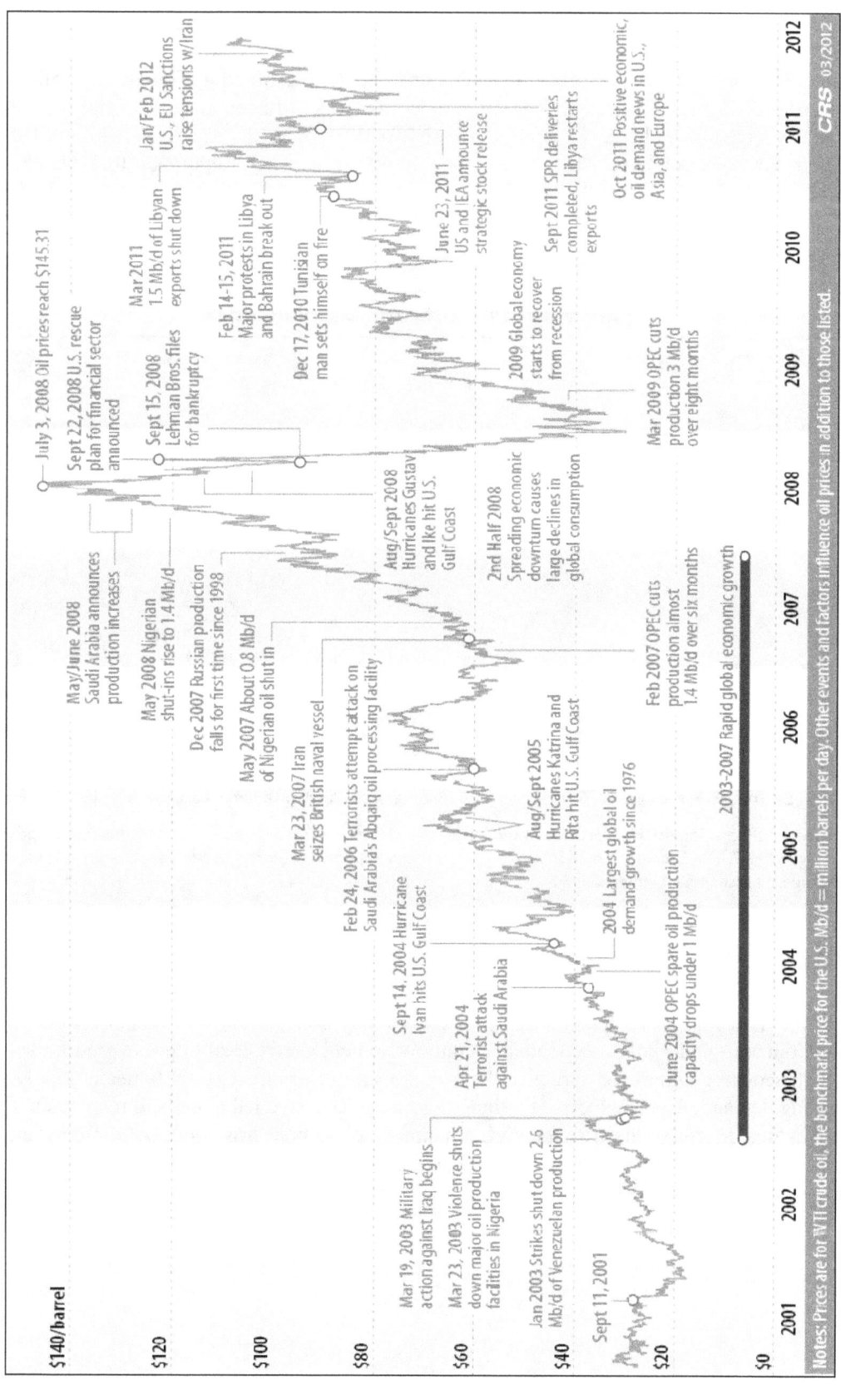

Notes: Prices are for WTI crude oil, the benchmark price for the U.S. Mb/d = million barrels per day. Other events and factors influence oil prices in addition to those listed.

Source: CRS and EIA.

Crude oil prices translate quickly into the prices for petroleum products. The primary determinant of gasoline price changes is the price of crude oil. According to EIA, the cost of crude oil made up about 76% of the cost of gasoline in December 2011. As illustrated in **Figure 6**, gasoline prices generally track the price of crude oil. Crude oil prices had been increasing from late 2011, particularly from November 2011 through March 2012. Gasoline price increases followed shortly thereafter. For background on what drives crude oil prices, see CRS Report R42024, *Oil Price Fluctuations*, by Neelesh Nerurkar and Mark Jickling. For more on 2012 increases in crude oil and petroleum product prices, see CRS Report R42382, *Rising Gasoline Prices 2012*, by Neelesh Nerurkar and Robert Pirog.

Figure 6. Crude Costs and Gasoline Prices

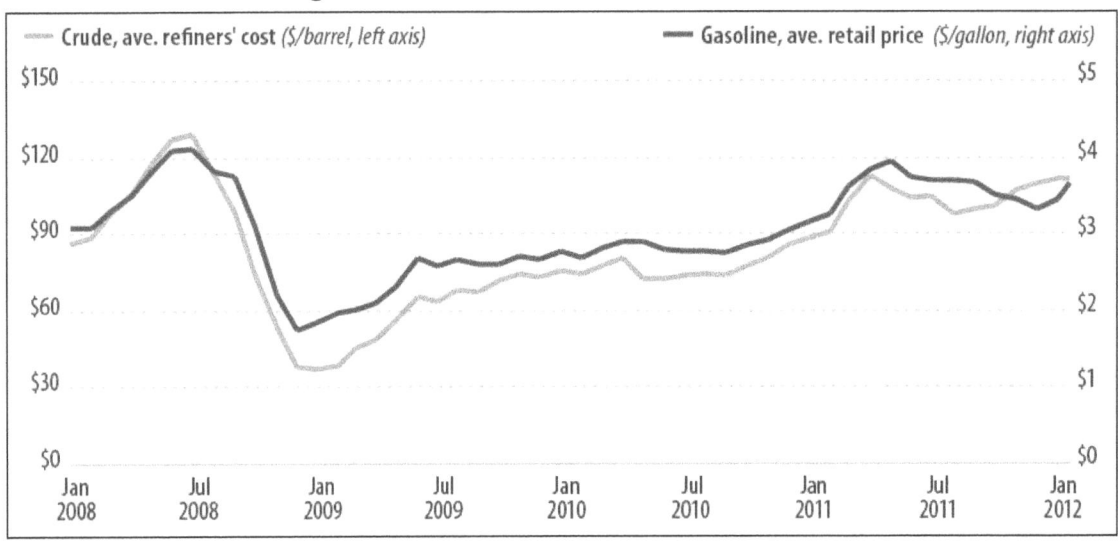

Data Source: EIA, *Petroleum & Other Liquid Fuels*, February 28, 2012, http://www.eia.gov/petroleum/data.cfm.

Notes: Refiners Acquisition Cost (RAC) of Crude until December 2012. 2012 values extrapolated based on changes in WTI. RAC data is a composite of domestic and imported crude oil costs. Gasoline price is national average, all grades, all formulations.

Policy Considerations

Oil import and export developments pose a host of policy issues, some of which are considered below. Concerns about import dependence continue to generate interest in policy options to directly discourage imports or to reduce the need for imports by increasing domestic supply and decreasing demand. Rising exports at a time of rising prices have led to calls to restrict such trade. The debate around the Keystone XL pipeline involves concerns about both imports and exports. Also discussed is the Strategic Petroleum Reserve, created to provide a short term policy option in case of supply disruptions at home or abroad.

Oil Import Policies

Shortly after the United States became a net oil importer, President Truman appointed the Paley Commission to examine the security of supply for oil and other basic materials. It supported policies for greater domestic production, particularly from oil shale,[21] and efficiency, but also advised against raising trade barriers to imports.[22] Imports continued to rise despite persistent concerns around import dependency. Under powers granted in the Trade Agreements Extension Act of 1958, President Eisenhower imposed quotas that limited imports east of the Rockies to a certain percentage of total consumption.[23] The quota program broke down by 1969 due to rising oil prices and quota loopholes. President Nixon replaced the program with an import fee in 1974, set at only a few cents per barrel.[24]

Current tariffs on oil imports range from 5.25¢ to 52.5¢ per barrel depending on the type of petroleum.[25] See various rates in the **Appendix**. Oil and petroleum products from certain countries are subject to duty-free treatment under several trade agreements and preferential trade programs enacted by Congress. The North American Free Trade Agreement (NAFTA), the Generalized System of Trade Preferences (GSP), and the African Growth and Opportunities Act (AGOA) account for most of the foregone revenue from waived tariffs.[26] At 2010 import levels, these and other waiver programs accounted for about $180 million dollars in foregone revenue, down from $215 million in 2005 when import volumes were higher.[27]

In the past, an increase in the tariff on oil has been considered a means to provide an advantage to domestic oil producers and reduce imports. Because tariffs on refined oil products are already at the highest levels permitted by U.S. agreements with the World Trade Organization (WTO), any

---

[21] Oil shale is a solid organic matter known as kerogen that is present in certain sedimentary rocks. The kerogen must be heated through different processes to convert it to a synthetic oil. This is different from shale oil (also referred to as "tight oil"), such as deposits in North Dakota's Bakken formation, which is fully formed oil trapped in low permeability rock. Oil shale remains too expensive to produce at scale, while shale/tight oil is being commercially extracted and growing rapidly, as discussed below in "Policies to Reduce the Need for Imports."

[22] The President's Materials Policy Commission, *Resources For Freedom*, July 2, 1952, p. 108.

[23] Mandatory Oil Import Program (MOIP), started in 1959, put a cap on how much foreign oil a refiner could import. Refiners were issued import allowance tickets that they could trade depending on their purchases of foreign oil. The program was managed to try to sustain domestic oil prices above $3/bbl.

[24] CRS Report RL30085, *Depressed Crude Oil Prices: Some Policy Options for Domestic Producers*, by Robert Bamberger, et al. (out of print).

[25] Except for petroleum-based lubricants, which have a tariff of 84¢/bbl.

[26] NAFTA is the free trade agreement between the United States, Mexico, and Canada. GSP is a U.S. program designed to promote economic growth in developing countries and includes about 131 beneficiary nations and territories. Originally created by the Trade Act of 1974, the GSP's authorization expired at the end of 2010. S. 308 has been introduced in the 112th Congress to reauthorize the GSP until June 12, 2012. It would apply retroactively to imports since December 31, 2011. Congress regularly reauthorizes GSP for short periods. The program had expired seven times between 1993 and 2002; each time it was reauthorized and applied retroactively for the lapsed period. See http://www.ustr.gov/webfm_send/2465. AGOA was enacted in 2000 to promote stable sustainable economic growth and development in Sub-Saharan Africa. It has a broader list of products than GSP that eligible countries may export to the United States that are subject to zero import duty. Oil accounts for more than 90% of AGOA imports—mostly from Nigeria and Angola, both OPEC members (http://www.agoa.gov/resources/US_African_Trade_Profile_2009.pdf).

[27] Data provided by the International Trade Administration. Forgone revenue estimate assumes a scenario where the same number of barrels would have been imported from countries with waivers if such waivers did not exist. This is an assumption. Although the tariff amount is small, it is possible that its absence could have shifted oil trade flows (e.g., that less oil would have been imported to the United States from these particular countries if waivers did not exist).

---

increase may be limited to crude oil tariffs.[28] The United States has not made any tariff commitments to the WTO binding duties on crude oil.[29] But like crude oil, refined products are globally traded. There is a risk that an increase in the tariff on crude oil alone may create a disadvantage for domestic refiners vis-à-vis their foreign competition by raising the cost of crude they use.[30] This could encourage more imports in the form of refined products instead of crude oil or discourage refined product exports—in either case potentially reducing refining capacity utilization at home.

Policies to Reduce the Need for Imports: Issues and Examples

The Obama Administration has targeted reducing oil imports by one-third over the next decade through encouraging greater conventional crude oil production, increased production of biofuels, efficiency improvements, and alternative fuel vehicles.[31] Members of Congress have introduced a range of proposals aimed at increasing domestic liquid fuels supply or reducing liquid fuels demand. These include creation of new policies or programs, or the removal of existing policy barriers to supply enhancing (or demand dampening) investment. Both sets of options come with associated costs and benefits to be weighed. This section briefly discusses several examples.

Increased Onshore Production

Larger components of recent domestic supply growth have come from onshore crude oil and natural gas liquids production (see **Table 1**). This has been driven in large part by greater production from tight oil and shale gas formations (shale gas formations can contain natural gas liquids, which are part of the oil market). Higher oil prices and advances in horizontal drilling and hydraulic fracturing technologies made these resources commercial. According to the International Energy Agency (IEA), U.S. tight oil production averaged 620,000 b/d in 2011, may grow to 870,000 b/d in 2012, and could reach 1.7 Mb/d by 2016.[32] About two-thirds of U.S. tight oil output in 2011 came from the Bakken and Three Forks deposits in North Dakota (see **Figure 7**). For context, the United States produced about 5.6 Mb/d of crude oil in 2011. Texas's Eagle Ford shale is another major source of tight oil production. There is also tight oil development in California and the Rockies. While particular forecasts differ, analysts generally expect significant growth in U.S. tight oil production going forward. However, there are environmental concerns around the processes used to extract these resources, including the impact on water resources and air quality.[33] State and federal government officials as well as industry are looking into how best

---

[28] U.S. President (Clinton), "The Uruguay Round Trade Agreements, Texts of Agreements Implementing Bill, Statement of Administrative Action and Required Supporting Statements," 103rd Cong., 2nd sess., September 27, 1994, 103-316, Vol 2 (Washington: GPO, 1994), pp. 2418-2422.

[29] Ibid, p. 2418.

[30] It would directly raise the cost of imported crude. It could also result in higher cost for the domestic crude they use as well since domestic producers could raise their price to that of now more expensive foreign imports.

[31] On March 30, 2011, the President announced the Administration's target to cut oil imports by one-third over a decade, relative to their levels when President Obama took office. If that baseline is 2008 annual average net imports, that value was 11.1 Mb/d. The developments described above have resulted in annual average net imports declining by about 24% between 2008 and 2011 (announcement at http://www.whitehouse.gov/the-press-office/2011/03/30/remarks-president-americas-energy-security).

[32] David Fyfe et al., *Oil Market Report (December, 2011)*, International Energy Agency, December 13, 2011, http://omrpublic.iea.org/omrarchive/13dec11full.pdf.

[33] Shale Gas Subcommittee of the Secretary of Energy Advisory Board, *The SEAB Shale Gas Production Subcommittee* (continued...)

---

to address these risks. For more, see CRS Report R42032, *The Bakken Formation: An Emerging Unconventional Oil Resource*, by Michael Ratner et al.

Figure 7. Bakken Crude Oil Production

Average monthly production

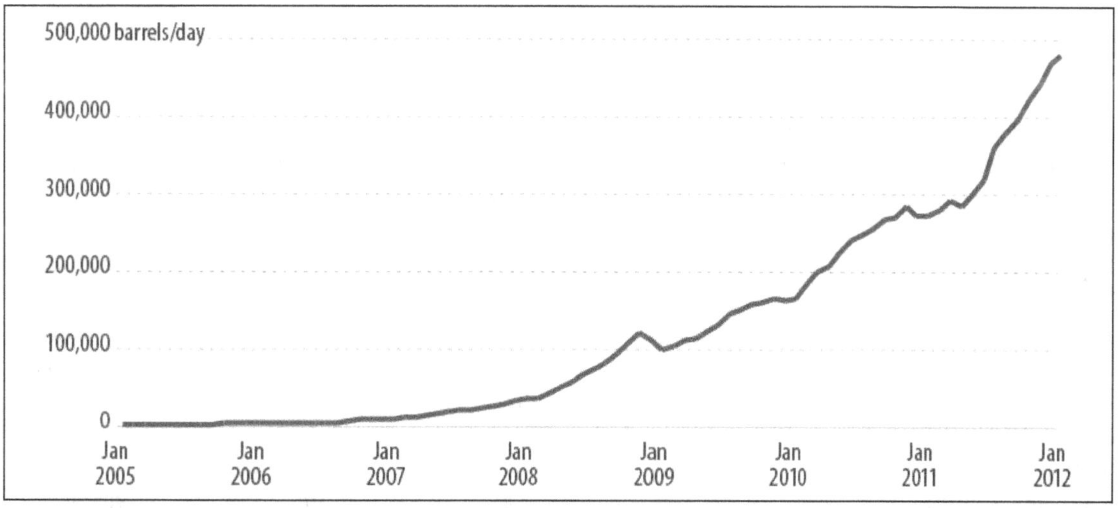

Source: North Dakota Department of Mineral Resources, *North Dakota's Bakken Oil Production Statistics*, https://www.dmr.nd.gov/oilgas/stats/historicalbakkenoilstats.pdf.

Notes: Includes Bakken, Sanish, Three Forks, and Bakken/Three Forks Pools.

Offshore Development

The tradeoffs surrounding offshore oil and gas development have been debated in recent years. Rising activity in progressively deeper and riskier waters, coupled with alleged industry and government complacency on safety, created environmental and worker safety risks that were realized with the Deepwater Horizon oil spill.[34] Risks to worker safety and the environment may be reduced with improved regulatory enforcement, new regulatory measures, or perhaps industry led preventative measures, though risks are not likely to be eliminated. As with tight oil development, state, federal, and industry officials are looking to incorporate practices which can mitigate these risks. For more, see CRS Report R42371, *Deepwater Horizon Oil Spill: Highlighted Activities*, by Jonathan L. Ramseur.

Alternative Fuels

Production and use of ethanol as a motor fuel is another example of policy tradeoffs. Fuel ethanol production has increased by roughly 0.7 Mb/d since 2005, when the Renewable Fuel Standard and ethanol excise tax credit were passed, and use of the alternative additive, Methyl tertiary butyl ether (MTBE), was phased out.[35] But some critics argue that increased use of corn for

---

(...continued)

Ninety-Day Report, August 18, 2011, http://www.shalegas.energy.gov/resources/081811_90_day_report_final.pdf.

[34] For more information on the Deepwater Horizon Oil Spill and issues for Congress, see CRS Report R41407, *Deepwater Horizon Oil Spill: Highlighted Actions and Issues* , by Curry L. Hagerty and Jonathan L. Ramseur.

[35] CRS Report R40110, *Biofuels Incentives: A Summary of Federal Programs*, by Brent D. Yacobucci.

biofuels has contributed to higher food prices. Others cite the high cost to taxpayers in the form of forgone revenues. The ethanol tax credit reduced federal excise tax revenue by roughly $6 billion in 2009; it cost taxpayers $1.78 for each gallon of gasoline consumption displaced by corn-based ethanol according to Congressional Budget Office estimates.[36] Further, there are limits to how much fuel ethanol can be absorbed by the U.S. market.[37] On December 31, 2011, most biofuels blending and production tax credits expired, with the exception of the cellulosic biofuels production tax credit, which is currently set to expire at the end of 2012.[38] For more, see CRS Report R41282, *Agriculture-Based Biofuels: Overview and Emerging Issues*, by Randy Schnepf.

There are also proposals to use coal and natural gas for transportation as a substitute for oil.[39] The United States is largely self-sufficient in these hydrocarbons due at least in part to large reserves of coal and growing natural gas resources. Many technologies that convert coal and natural gas to liquid fuels or otherwise make it possible to use them in transportation tend to be expensive and require large investments in processing facilities, infrastructure, and/or investment in vehicles. To the extent this is resolved with federal support, there is a fiscal trade-off. Further, there are concerns that coal-to-liquids technology emits significant amounts of greenhouse gases. Natural gas technology options also emit greenhouse gases though less so than coal. Growing natural gas supplies and low domestic natural gas prices have made these technologies more attractive. However, there are competing uses for natural gas, including use in power generation, domestic industry,[40] and interest by some in exporting it overseas as liquefied natural gas (LNG) to countries with higher natural gas prices.[41] LNG exports have to be approved by the Department of Energy. As of February 28, 2011, the Department of Energy had received 10 applications for LNG facilities with a collective export capacity of 13.8 billion cubic feet per day, equivalent to about 22% of 2011 U.S. dry gas production.[42]

For more on alternative fuels, including biofuels, natural gas vehicles, and electric vehicles, see CRS Report R40168, *Alternative Fuels and Advanced Technology Vehicles: Issues in Congress*, by Brent D. Yacobucci.

Improving Efficiency

There are also demand-side examples of policy trade-offs. Congress increased the Corporate Average Fuel Economy standard (CAFE) in 2007,[43] its first increase for cars in two decades.

---

[36] Congressional Budget Office, *Using Biofuel Tax Credits to Achieve Energy and Environmental Policy Goals*, July 2010, http://www.cbo.gov/ftpdocs/114xx/doc11477/07-14-Biofuels.pdf.

[37] CRS Report R40445, *Intermediate-Level Blends of Ethanol in Gasoline, and the Ethanol "Blend Wall"*, by Brent D. Yacobucci.

[38] For more about biofuels growth and related federal policy, see CRS Report R41282, *Agriculture-Based Biofuels: Overview and Emerging Issues*, by Randy Schnepf.

[39] For instance, provisions in the New Alternative Transportation to Give Americans Solutions Act of 2011 (H.R. 1380 and S. 1863) and Roadmap for America's Energy Future (H.R. 909).

[40] CRS Report R41628, *Industrial Demand and the Changing Natural Gas Market*, by Robert Pirog.

[41] CRS Report R42074, *U.S. Natural Gas Exports: New Opportunities, Uncertain Outcomes*, by Michael Ratner, Paul W. Parfomak, and Linda Luther.

[42] Office of Fossil Energy, U.S. Department of Energy, *Summary of LNG Export Applications*, February 28, 2012, http://www.fossil.energy.gov/programs/gasregulation/LNG_Export_Concise_Summary_03_01_12.pdf. Domestic dry gas production in 2011 was 63.0 bcf/d. For more on this issue, see CRS Report R42074, *U.S. Natural Gas Exports: New Opportunities, Uncertain Outcomes*, by Michael Ratner, Paul W. Parfomak, and Linda Luther.

[43] P.L. 110-140, Sec. 102.

Proposed regulations under CAFE standards would gradually raise the average fuel economy of new passenger cars and light trucks each year to reach a combined 49.6 miles per gallon (mpg) by 2025.[44] This has played an important role in expectations for lower oil imports over the next several decades, but effects of higher CAFE standards can take years to manifest because it takes years to turn over the vehicle fleet. To spur growth in the auto industry and accelerate vehicle efficiency, Congress passed the Consumer Assistance to Recycle and Save Act of 2009 (CARS, also known as "Cash-for-Clunkers") which provided a $3,500 or $4,500 rebate for trading in a used car for a more fuel efficient vehicle (the amount depended on the fuel economy improvement).[45] According to the Council on Economic Advisors, the CARS program provided a temporary stimulus that contributed to economic recovery from recession,[46] created jobs,[47] and likely reduced some fuel consumption faster than CAFE. But there were trade-offs: Accelerating fuel efficiency through CARS may have cost the government significantly more than the estimated future fuel savings for participating consumers.[48] It may only reduce 2020 oil consumption and greenhouse gas emissions by an estimated 0.02%.[49] It accelerated some sales that would have taken place in future months anyway.[50] And by scrapping cars traded in, it may have increased the cost of vehicles for those who purchase used cars in the future.

Export Restrictions on Crude Oil and Petroleum Products

Crude Oil Export Restrictions

Crude oil exports are generally prohibited by statute. The Energy Policy and Conservation Act of 1975 (P.L. 94-163, EPCA) directs the President to restrict the export of crude oil.[51] There are also additional restrictions on export of crude oil transported on pipelines that received federal right of

---

[44] Separately, it is 56.0 mpg for passenger cars and 40.3 mpg for light trucks. Environmental Protection Agency and the National Highway Traffic Safety Administration, "2017 and Later Model Year Light-Duty Vehicle Greenhouse Gas Emissions and Corporate Average Fuel Economy Standards," 76 *Federal Register* 74954, December 1, 2011.

[45] P.L. 111-32, Secs. 1301 and 1302.

[46] The United States was in recession from December 2007 until June 2009. Council of Economic Advisors estimated that CARS raised third quarter 2009 gross domestic product (GDP) growth by around 0.2 percentage points (annualized rate). Council of Economic Advisers, "Economic Analysis of the Car Allowance Rebate System," September 10, 2009, p. 12.

[47] Ibid, p. 13.

[48] According to National Highway Traffic Safety Administration (NHTSA), CARS cost approximately $3.0 billion, but provided future fuel savings for consumers who participated of only an expected $1.3 to $1.9 billion (based on applying a 7% and a 3% discount rate respectively to calculate present value of future savings). NHTSA, *Consumer Assistance to Recycle and Save Act of 2009: Report to the House Committee on Energy and Commerce, the Senate Committee on Commerce, Science, and Transportation and the House and Senate Committees on* Appropriations, December 2009, p. 46, http://www.cars.gov/files/official-information/CARS-Report-to-Congress.pdf.

This may still be the case even if one assumes a cost of the greenhouse gas emissions avoided: assuming $20 per ton, CARS saved another roughly $0.2 billion through avoided emissions (p. 49). The value of reducing other air pollutants was estimated at $0.2 billion (p. 53). Critics pointed out that the program could have been more cost effective had it required a wider difference in the fuel efficiency between cars traded in and new cars purchased.

[49] CRS Report R40654, *Accelerated Vehicle Retirement for Fuel Economy: "Cash for Clunkers"*, by Brent D. Yacobucci and Bill Canis.

[50] Edmunds.com, "Cash for Clunkers Results Finally In: Taxpayers Paid $24,000 per Vehicle Sold, Report Edmunds.com," October 28, 2009.

[51] 42 U.S.C. § 6212.

---

ways,[52] produced on the outer continental shelf,[53] or produced from the Naval Petroleum Reserve.[54] There are certain cases where crude oil exports are permitted in statute: If it is shipped on the Trans-Alaska Pipeline, of foreign origin, or is from the Strategic Petroleum Reserve if such export will directly result in import of refined products not otherwise available.

The Department of Commerce's Bureau of Industry and Security (BIS), which regulates crude oil exports under its Short Supply Controls, will grant export licenses for crude oil that fall into these categories above.[55] They would otherwise not be granted. While infrequent, there are instances where crude of foreign origin is shipped into the United States and then re-exported. If the crude is of foreign origin and has not been co-mingled with crude of U.S. origin, it may be permitted for export.[56]

EPCA and other statutes allow the President to permit crude oil export in circumstances where the President determines that such exports are in the national interest. The President made such determinations for limited export of heavy crude oil from California in 1992,[57] crude oil produced from Alaska's Cook Inlet in 1985,[58] and oil exports to Canada for use or consumption therein in 1985 and 1988.[59] In 1995, Congress passed P.L. 104-58 which amended the Mineral Leasing Act to permit exports of oil carried on the Trans-Alaska pipeline unless the President determined that these exports are not in the national interest. It directed the President to make such a determination within five months of the bill's passage. The President issued a determination that such exports were in the national interest. Small amounts of crude oil were exported from Alaska until 2000, when changing commercial factors made exports uneconomic.[60]

Refined Product Exports

Export of refined petroleum products are generally permitted and do not require a license from BIS.[61] EPCA does not require the President to restrict refined products exports the way it does crude oil, though it does grant the President the authority to restrict exports of coal, petroleum products, natural gas, or petrochemical feedstock "by rule, under such terms and conditions as he determines to be appropriate and necessary to carry out the purposes of this Act."[62] This authority has never been utilized. In recent months, policy makers have expressed interest in restricting petroleum product exports as their export volumes have risen and petroleum product prices have also gone up.

---

[52] 30 U.S.C. § 185(u).

[53] 29 U.S.C. § 1354.

[54] 10 U.S.C. § 7430.

[55] 15 C.F.R. § 754.2

[56] *De minimus* mingling as an inevitable result of shared infrastructure, such as pipelines and storage tanks, is likely to be excused.

[57] 3 C.F.R. 382 1992.

[58] 51 FR 20252.

[59] 54 F.R. 271 and 50 F.R. 25189.

[60] CRS Report RS22142, *West Coast and Alaska Oil Exports*, by Lawrence Kumins.

[61] The exception is for petroleum products derived from crude oil produced from the Naval Petroleum Reserve. (15 CFR 754.3).

[62] 42 U.S.C. 6212 (a).

U.S. international trade commitments may limit the ability to prohibit exports if an export prohibition cannot be justified under an available trade agreement exception. The General Agreement on Tariffs and Trade (GATT), to which the United States is a signatory, prohibits WTO Members from maintaining quantitative prohibitions or restrictions, such as quotas, on the exportation of any product to another WTO Member country. (While issues differ, it may be worth noting that the United States recently requested consultations with China under the WTO Dispute Settlement Understanding over Chinese export restrictions on rare earth elements, which are used in energy and other applications, and successfully challenged China in the WTO over its export restrictions on a variety of raw materials.[63]) There is an exception to the GATT prohibition on export restrictions for temporary measures to prevent critical shortages of foodstuffs or other essential products. The GATT also contains general exceptions including those for measures relating to the conservation of exhaustible natural resources if imposed in conjunction with limits on domestic production or consumption, export restrictions posed in conjunction with price stabilization plans, and restrictions for reasons of short supply.[64] Separately, Article 605 of the North American Free Trade Agreement (NAFTA) places additional restrictions on the ability of the United States to limit exports of energy and basic petrochemical goods to Canada and vice versa (Mexico is not party to Article 605). Both GATT and NAFTA contain national security exceptions, though NAFTA limits the scope of the exceptions for the United States and Canada in energy trade (see NAFTA, Article 607).[65]

To what degree prohibiting petroleum product exports would reduce prices is unclear. Some contend that there may be a decline in the price of gasoline and other refined products if their export were restricted. Others suggest there will be no decline in gasoline prices if such measures were adopted.[66] Export proponents point out that the import of relatively less expensive crude oil and the export of relatively more expensive refined products can support economic growth.

Without the option to export, refiners that had been exporting petroleum products may either find a way to sell additional volumes within the United States or operate their refineries at lower levels of capacity utilization. The former option requires refiners to discount products and accept lower margins to sell products into the domestic market. (Presumably they are currently able to sell products at higher prices abroad than the lower prices that would be necessary to market more products domestically). The degree to which this can take place is limited by the latter—if refiners cannot buy crude, process it, and sell products at a profit, they will curtail operations.[67] Oil consumption is relatively "inelastic" (unresponsive) to price and more responsive to income

---

[63] Request for Consultations by the United States, China—Measures Related to the Exportation of Rare Earths, Tungsten and Molybdenum, WT/DS431/1 (March 15, 2012); Appellate Body Report, China—Measures Related to the Exportation of Various Raw Materials, WT/DS394/AB/R, WT/DS395/AB/R, WT/DS398/AB/R (January 30, 2012). Chinese export restrictions on raw materials were also successfully challenged by the European Union (EU) and Mexico. Japan and the EU have also requested consultations with China regarding its export restrictions on rare earths; in addition, Canada has asked to join the consultations in each of the three proceedings.

[64] Article XX(g),(i),(j). Note that Article XX contains a proviso requiring that measures justified under these exceptions not arbitrarily or unjustifiably discriminate between countries where the same conditions prevail (including between the exporting and the importing country) or constitute a disguised restriction on international trade.

[65] For more on this, see CRS Congressional Distribution Memorandum "Possible Trade Agreement Implications of Import and Export Restrictions on Oil and Natural Gas," by Jeanne Grimmett. Available by request.

[66] American Petroleum Institute, "More Domestic Oil Key to Addressing Higher Gasoline Prices," press release, February 22, 2012, http://www.api.org/news-and-media/news/newsitems/2012/feb-2012/more-domestic-oil-key-to-addressing-higher-gasoline-prices.aspx.

[67] Crude oil is an input to refining, so higher crude prices represent higher costs to refiners, not profits—though they may represent higher profits for the upstream arm of integrated oil companies that both produce crude and refine it.

---

and economic growth: It may take large discounts in price to sell additional volumes, especially into a weak economy. Some may argue that sufficient discounts may be uneconomic for export-restricted refiners to carry out, and that such refiners would instead curtail production. While how this may play out is uncertain, what is clear is that any impact on product prices would be bounded by the price of crude oil, which is the main driver of higher gasoline, diesel, and other refined product prices.[68]

As with international trade concerns in other goods and services, concerns about petroleum products exports can be thought of as a distributional issue. It is likely a benefit to the economy if existing refining capacity can be utilized in a way which contributes to export earnings. Rising petroleum product exports shown in **Table 7** helped mitigate the increase in the net oil import bill. On average, petroleum products are likely to have higher prices than the crude from which they are refined.[69] That economic benefit may accrue to refiners to the degree they have invested in refining capacity and have beneficial access to crude supplies and export markets. Consumers may face higher costs when foreign markets are willing to pay more for refined products. However, the benefit to consumers from prohibiting exports may be limited—the price of gasoline and other refined products is largely driven by crude oil prices. And restricting U.S. exports may mean that foreign markets which would be served by U.S. refiners are instead served by foreign refining capacity and U.S. refiners curtail utilization of existing capacity.

Oil Export Tariff

Instead of prohibiting exports, some have suggested a federal tax, tariff, or duty on exports. However, these are generally prohibited by Article 1, section 9, clause 5 of the U.S. Constitution, which states that "No Tax or Duty shall be laid on articles exported from any State."[70]

The Keystone XL Pipeline and Oil Trade

Both proponents and opponents of the proposed Keystone XL pipeline have cited the impact on U.S. oil trade among their arguments. Proponents argue that Keystone XL would facilitate greater production from Canada's oil sands and import of that supply by the United States, where it could substitute for oil from less reliable sources. Some also contend that, absent such a pipeline into the United States, oil sands production may grow more slowly than might otherwise be the case and/or that infrastructure may be built that would allow rising oil sands output to go to Asia in addition to the United States.

Opposition to the pipeline stems from concerns about environmental impacts,[71] but opponents also question the economic and energy security benefits of the project. Among the trade-related issues argued by the pipeline's opponents is the contention that crude oil from the pipeline may be

---

[68] CRS Report R42382, *Rising Gasoline Prices 2012*, by Neelesh Nerurkar and Robert Pirog.

[69] At times the value of some lower end products may be less than the price of crude, but the activity may be made economically viable by higher margins for products such as diesel for which there is strong global demand. Refiners can adjust their output to a degree, but are limited in how much they can gear their production toward certain products. Many refineries may have already maximized diesel output in the current market environment.

[70] See generally Congressional Research Service, *The Constitution of the United States of America: Analysis and Interpretation*, pp. 375-376, 2004.

[71] For more on environmental issues and general background, see CRS Report R41668, *Keystone XL Pipeline Project: Key Issues*, by Paul W. Parfomak et al.

exported to other countries rather than remain in the United States. Alternatively, others have suggested that the crude oil may be refined in the United States and the products exported. They also contend that Keystone XL will not insulate the United States from price fluctuations that raise import costs.

Background on Keystone XL

In 2008, Canadian pipeline company TransCanada filed an application with the U.S. Department of State to build the Keystone XL pipeline, which would transport crude oil from the oil sands region of Alberta, Canada, to refineries on the U.S. Gulf Coast. Keystone XL would ultimately have the capacity to transport 830,000 barrels per day, delivering crude oil to the market hub at Cushing, OK, and further to points in Texas. TransCanada plans to build a pipeline spur so that oil from the Bakken formation in Montana and North Dakota can also be carried on Keystone XL.

As a facility connecting the United States with a foreign country, the pipeline requires a Presidential Permit from the State Department. In evaluating such a permit application, after consultation with other relevant federal agencies and public input, the department must determine whether a proposal is in the "national interest." This determination considers the project's potential effects on the environment, economy, energy security, foreign policy, and other factors. Pursuant to the National Environmental Policy Act, the State Department considered potential environmental impacts of the proposed Keystone XL project in a final Environmental Impact Statement (EIS) issued on August 26, 2011. A wide range of public comments both for and against the pipeline were received during a subsequent 90-day review period. The State Department noted, in particular, concerns about the pipeline's route through the Sand Hills region of Nebraska, an extensive sand dune formation with highly porous soil and shallow groundwater.

The Temporary Payroll Tax Cut Continuation Act of 2011 (P.L. 112-78) included provisions requiring the Secretary of State to issue a permit for the project within 60 days unless the President determined the project not to be in the national interest. On January 18, 2012, the State Department, with the President's consent, denied the Keystone XL permit, citing insufficient time under the 60-day deadline to obtain all the necessary information to assess the reconfigured project. On February 27, 2012, TransCanada announced that it would proceed with development of the Keystone XL segment connecting Cushing, OK, to the Gulf Coast as a stand-alone project not requiring a Presidential Permit. The company also informed the State Department that it intended to file a new Presidential Permit application "in the near future" for the segment of the Keystone XL project from the Canadian border to Steele City, NE, with a future supplement to the application specifying an alternative route in Nebraska. The company has stated that it expects to establish the new route by October 2012. The Obama Administration supports TransCanada's plan to proceed with the southernmost segment of the Keystone XL pipeline while reserving judgment on a reconfigured northern segment until completion of a new Presidential Permit review.

For more on Keystone XL, including environmental concerns, domestic market impacts, and recent legislation, see CRS Report R41668, *Keystone XL Pipeline Project: Key Issues*, by Paul W. Parfomak et al., from which this summary is taken.

Export and Import Issues

It appears possible that Canadian crude oil traveling through the United States via a pipeline such as Keystone XL may receive a license to be exported from the United States. As discussed above, EPCA allows for export of foreign origin crude.[72] The Mineral Leasing Act's restriction on export of crude traveling through pipelines that receive federal rights of way applies to domestically produced crude.[73] However, given the U.S. Gulf Coast's large concentration of sophisticated refining capacity and large need for foreign crude, it may be more economic to refine Canadian crude from the oil sands in the United States. Most of the crude imported from the oil sands today and most of the growth in oil sands production is expected to be in the form of a heavy sour crude which requires sophisticated refining capacity to be processed in large quantities.[74] Heavy sour

---

[72] See "Export Restrictions on Crude Oil and Petroleum Products."

[73] 30 U.S.C. 185(u).

[74] Canadian Association of Petroleum Producers, "Crude Oil Forecast, Markets & Pipelines," June 2011, http://www.capp.ca/forecast/Pages/default.aspx.

crude from Canada's oil sands will presumably compete with foreign seaborne heavy sour crudes, which could be diverted elsewhere. Foreign seaborne sources of U.S. heavy sour crude imports include Brazil, Colombia, Ecuador, Kuwait, Mexico, Peru, Russia, the United Kingdom, and Venezuela.[75] According to a report commissioned by the Department of Energy, if pipeline capacity from the oil sands to the United States is not built and if Canada expands pipeline capacity to its west coast, this may result in growing oil sands output being shipped to Asia and leave the United States importing correspondingly more oil from the Middle East and Africa.[76] It is not certain if projects expanding pipeline capacity to Canada's West Coast will be carried out. They face opposition from environmental and First Nations groups, though the Canadian federal government has announced plans to streamline the environmental review process for such projects.[77]

A separate issue is if the Canadian crude will be refined into petroleum products that may then be exported. It is possible that some of the petroleum products refined from crude oil carried on the Keystone XL pipeline may be exported. There is no existing policy that would restrict these exports. Petroleum product exports have been commercially attractive in recent years, as described above. U.S. petroleum product exports have come predominately from the Gulf Coast region to which Keystone XL would carry crude oil. It is difficult to predict to what degree this may occur. Legislation that would prohibit export of petroleum products refined from oil that travels through Keystone XL has been introduced.[78] Implementation of such measures may be complicated by how refineries can process multiple crudes. There may also be a conflict with U.S. commitments under international trade agreements (see "Export Restrictions on Crude Oil and Petroleum Products"). Even if some portion of Canadian crude carried on Keystone XL is refined and exported, it may still displace foreign imports from elsewhere if, in the absence of Keystone XL, refiners would have imported crude from elsewhere for refining and export.

Oil Prices

Keystone XL will not insulate the United States from global oil price fluctuations. However, if it facilitates greater global oil supply, it may contribute to global oil prices being lower than they might otherwise be.

The proposed pipeline would connect oil sands production and tight oil production in North Dakota to the Midwest oil hub of Cushing, OK, and to refineries in the Gulf Coast. This addresses three current or potential future transportation bottlenecks: between the oil sands and United States, between growing oil supplies in North Dakota and other markets, and between the Midwest and the Gulf Coast. Regarding the first, according to some estimates there is currently sufficient pipeline capacity between Canada and the United States to handle growing imports

---

[75] Countries from which the United States imported 12 or more cargos of crude with less than 23 API and greater than 0.5% sulfur content in 2010 according to EIA (http://www.eia.gov/petroleum/imports/companylevel/). Of these sources, the only sources of crude with sulfur content of greater than 3% were Venezuela, Kuwait, Colombia, and Mexico (along with Canada, whose crude imports are primarily by pipeline).

[76] EnSys Energy & Systems, Inc., *Keystone XL Assessment: Final Report*, Prepared for the U.S. Department of Energy, Office of Policy & International Affairs, December 23, 2010, p. 118, http://www.keystonepipeline-xl.state.gov/clientsite/keystonexl.nsf/AssmtDrftAccpt.pdf.

[77] "Ottawa to eases pipeline rules in bid to boost oil exports to Asia," *Financial Post*, March 30, 2012.

[78] For instance, H.R. 3900 [112th].

---

until around 2019.[79] The transport issues regarding growing North Dakota production are currently a concern but fall beyond the scope of this report.[80] The third bottleneck is currently an issue for oil sands and U.S. Midwestern crude oil producers. Rising production from these sources and the limited southbound crude pipeline capacity has resulted in a glut of crudes in the Midwest market. This has benefited Midwestern refiners who can purchase discounted crude but can charge Midwestern consumers petroleum product prices in line with the national average.[81] This bottleneck between the Midwest and Gulf Coast is expected to be alleviated in part by the reversal of the Seaway pipeline, which runs between Oklahoma and the Texas coast (expected this summer), so that it will run from north to south. It may further be addressed by TransCanada's plans to build the southernmost leg of the originally proposed Keystone XL pipeline, now referred to as the Gulf Coast Pipeline Project, which would run a similar route to Seaway.

Reaching a larger market for crude oil, beyond the Midwest, with a larger amount of sophisticated refining capacity (such as the Gulf Coast), may reduce the discount oil sands crudes currently face in the Midwest. Even if there is currently available pipeline capacity into the United States, oil sands (and pipeline) projects take years to plan and build, and investment decisions may be based at least in part on expected transport options. If greater certainty about transport options results in greater investment and more rapid development in the oil sands, it could raise global oil supply and contribute to oil prices being lower than might otherwise be the case.[82] At maximum capacity, Keystone XL could carry about 0.8 Mb/d, which is about 1% of today's roughly 89 Mb/d global oil market. This would represent a 20% increase in the existing pipeline capacity carrying oil from Canada to the United States.[83] It is unclear to what degree this additional pipeline transport capacity could facilitate faster or greater production growth from the oil sands, and to what extent that will contribute to lower global prices. Some may argue that the increment would be too small to make a substantial difference in oil prices given the size of the global oil market. However, it may be worth noting that most individual energy production and infrastructure projects—whether they involve conventional, unconventional, alternative, or renewable energy—when measured in isolation will look small relative to the global oil market.

Global crude oil prices will still experience fluctuations.[84] However, when oil prices rise, it may be less economically harmful to the United States if more of the resulting wealth transfer from oil importers to oil exporters went to countries that are major trade partners and may be more likely to spend growing wealth on U.S. goods and services.

---

[79] Testimony of Jim Burkhard, IHS CERA for the U.S. Congress, Senate Committee on Energy and Natural Resources, US and Global Energy Outlook for 2012, 112th Cong., 2nd sess., January 31, 2012.

[80] See CRS Report R42032, *The Bakken Formation: An Emerging Unconventional Oil Resource*, by Michael Ratner et al.

[81] The Midwest still brings in petroleum products from the Gulf Coast region.

[82] For an explanation of how supply affects oil prices, see CRS Report R42024, *Oil Price Fluctuations*, by Neelesh Nerurkar and Mark Jickling.

[83] CRS Report R41875, *The U.S.-Canada Energy Relationship: Joined at the Well*, by Paul W. Parfomak and Michael Ratner.

[84] Ibid.

Greenhouse Gas Emissions from Oil Sands and Other Crudes[85]

Benefits of increased oil supply from Canadian oil sands may be weighed against environmental costs. Of particular concern to some have been the greenhouse gas (GHG) emissions that may result from greater production, import, and use of oil sands crudes. A number of studies have found that the GHG emissions of oil sands crudes may be higher than for the average crude oil used in the United States. Results between studies vary due to differences in data, methodology, and how they are specified. Many studies are "Well-to-Wheels" (WTW) life-cycle assessments (LCAs), which include emissions of carbon and other GHG emissions from crude extraction, transportation, refining, distribution of refined product to retail markets, and the combustion of the fuel by end users (e.g., in vehicles or factories). Other studies focus on only part of the supply chain, for instance studies that are "Well-to-Tank" or "Well-to-Refinery Gate." Final combustion can represent 70%-80% of WTW emissions of any crude, so its exclusion in an LCA can make a significant difference on how much more GHG intensive oil sands crudes appear in a study's results. Beyond just stages, what inputs into fuel production should be included in a full LCA, as well as the values and weights of those inputs is a matter of ongoing debate.

While GHG emissions and other air quality issues originating in the upstream (extraction) sectors of Canada's petroleum industry do not directly impact U.S. National Emissions Inventories or U.S. GHG reporting per se, many environmental stakeholders and policymakers have noted that increased use of more GHG-intensive resources in the United States may have negative consequences for both U.S. and global energy policy and environmental practices as the location of GHG emissions is far less relevant than the total global emissions. The U.S. Department of State, in response to comments on the draft Environmental Impact Statement (EIS) for the Keystone XL pipeline project, investigated the GHG life-cycle emissions associated with these resources in comparison to other reference crudes. The Department of State presented this analysis in the Final EIS as a "matter of policy," but noted that an EIS was not required to include an assessment of environmental activities outside the United States.[86] Further, it stated that while the proposed Keystone XL pipeline project may contribute to certain continental scale environmental impacts, it may not substantially influence either the rate or magnitude of oil extraction activities in Canada or the overall volume of crude oil transported to and refined in the United States. The Final EIS concluded that, despite differences in study designs and input assumptions, the crudes that would likely be transported on the proposed Keystone XL pipeline, are on average "somewhat more GHG-intensive than the crudes they would displace in the U.S. refineries."[87]

---

[85] This section based on work by CRS Analyst Rick Lattanzio.

[86] The Department of State noted that this was not required by the National Environmental Policy Act (NEPA) nor Department of State regulations (22 CFR 161.12) nor Executive Orders 13337 and 12114 (Environmental Effects Abroad of Major Federal Activities).

[87] Department of State, Final Environmental Impact Statement, Keystone XL Project, 3.14-56.

Figure 8. NETL Well-to-Wheel GHG Emissions Estimates for Selected U.S. Crude Imports

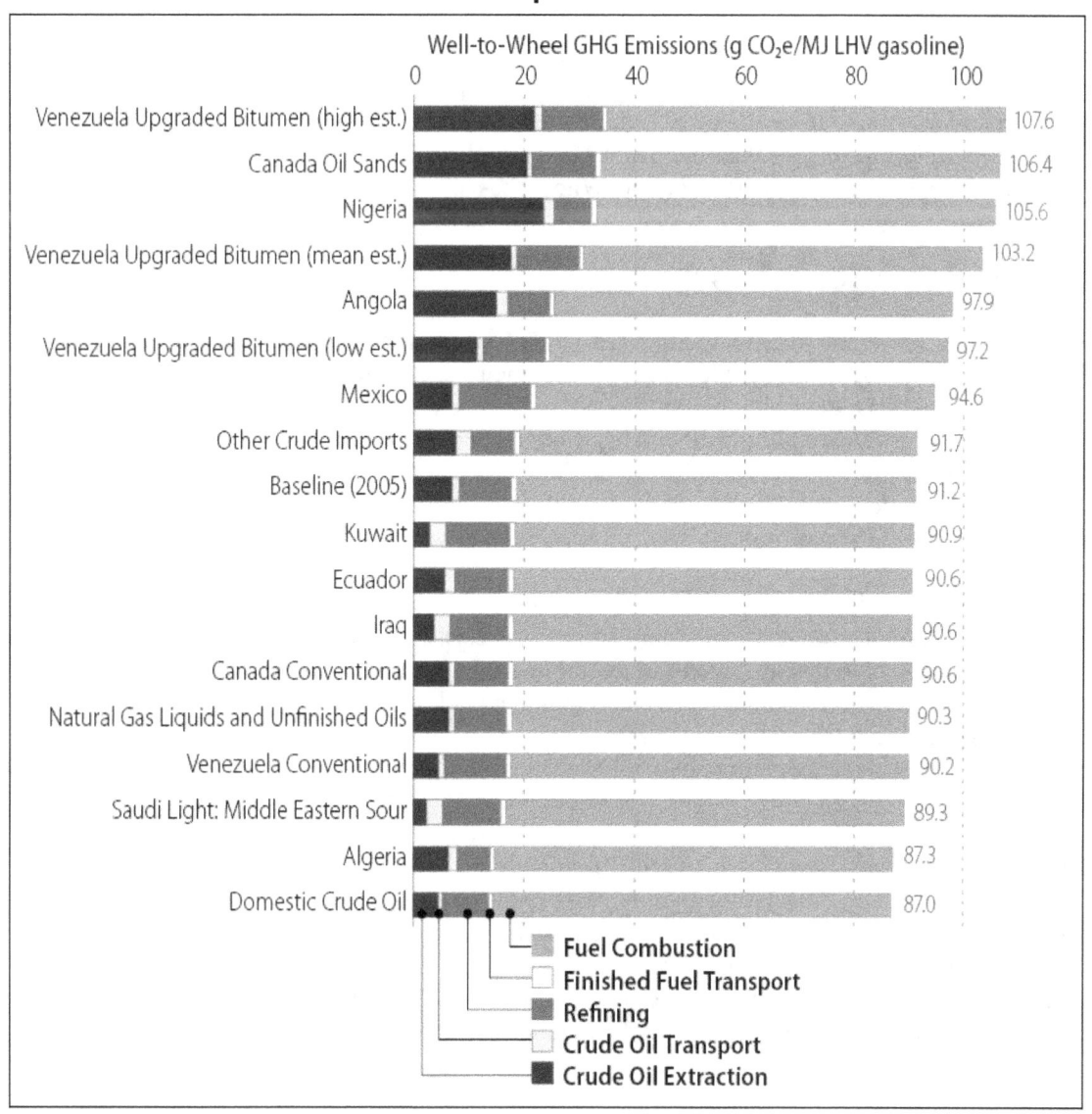

Source: CRS, from *An Evaluation of the Extraction, Transport and Refining of Imported Crude Oils and the Impact of Life Cycle Greenhouse Gas Emissions*, National Energy Technology Laboratory, March 27, 2009.

Notes: NETL values converted from kgCO2e/MMBtu using conversion factors of 1,055 MJ/MMBtu and 1000 g/kg. NETL input assumptions are as follows: (1) Assumes a weighted average of WCSB oil sands extraction at 43% raw bitumen (not accounting for blending with diluents to form dilbit) from Cyclic Steam Stimulation in-situ production and 57% Synthetic Crude Oil from mining production in the years 2005 and 2006; (2) Allocates refinery emissions from co-products other than the gasoline, diesel, and jet fuel to the co-products themselves, including petroleum coke, and thus outside the boundaries of the LCA (unless combusted at refinery); (3) Uses linear relationships to relate GHG emissions from refining operations based on API gravity and sulfur content, thus failing to fully account for the various produced residuum ranges of bitumen blends and SCO; (4) Does not fully evaluate the impact of pre-refining SCO at the upgrader prior to the refinery; (5) Does not account for the transportation emissions of co-products; and (6) Bounds the GHG emissions estimates for Venezuela's ultra-heavy oil/bitumen using uncertainty analysis due to the limited availability of public data.

The findings of a 2009 National Energy Technology Laboratory (NETL) study, which estimates the WTW GHG emissions of producing gasoline from various crudes, is presented in **Figure 8**.

According to the NETL study, producing and consuming gasoline from a weighted average of Canadian oil sands crudes imported into the United States yields about 17% more GHG gasoline derived from the average mix of crudes used in the United States in 2005 ("baseline"). However, it is comparable to gasoline derived from U.S. imports of some Venezuelan and Nigerian crudes. Across the various published studies analyzed by the Department of State, fuel produced from oil sands crudes was found to be 9% to 19% more GHG-intensive than fuel from Middle Eastern heavy sour crude, 5% to 13% than fuel from Mexican Maya crude, and 2% to 6% than fuel from Venezuelan Bachaquero crude on a Well-to-Wheels basis.[88]

Strategic Petroleum Reserve

In the wake of the Arab Oil Embargo in 1973-1974, Congress created Strategic Petroleum Reserve (SPR), a stockpile of crude oil to mitigate the impact of future supply disruptions. The SPR currently holds 696 million barrels of oil, 96% of its total storage capacity, in five salt dome caverns located in Texas and Louisiana. This is equivalent to 83 days' worth of U.S. net oil imports. At its maximum rate, the SPR can be draw down at 4.25 Mb/d for 90 days; the rate diminishes thereafter.[89] The President has the authority to release oil from the SPR in the event of "severe energy supply interruptions."

Also in response to the Arab Oil Embargo, the United States joined with other advanced economies to form the International Energy Agency (IEA). IEA members have pledged to hold oil stocks equivalent to 90 days' worth of net oil imports (includes government held and commercial stocks). As of January 2012, IEA members held more than 4 billion barrels of oil stocks, of which 1.5 billion were government controlled.[90] IEA government held stocks could be brought to market at a maximum rate of 14.4 Mb/d in the first month of an IEA collective action.[91]

The United States has drawn down the SPR for emergency reasons in three cases of global supply disruptions, each in coordination with other IEA countries: Iraq's invasion of Kuwait and the subsequent Gulf War (1990/91), Hurricanes Katrina and Rita in the U.S. Gulf Coast (2005), and after prolonged disruption of Libyan exports (2011). These events reduced global oil supply. As described above, that can affect oil prices around the world, including the cost of U.S. domestic oil and oil imports, even if these imports do not come from the disrupted sources. These releases

[88] Done in conjunction with the consultancy firm IFC International LLC (IFC). The full report by IFC is presented as Appendix V of the Final EIS: IFC International LLC, "Life-Cycle Greenhouse Gas Emissions of Petroleum Products from WCSB Oil Sands Crudes Compared with Reference Crudes," July 13, 2011.

[89] According to the Department of Energy, the maximum rate as of March 2012 was 4.25 Mb/d, down from 4.4 Mb/d because one storage tank for loading vessels with SPR crude is in need of repair. According to reports, some analysts argue that distribution capacity may be lower than this due to infrastructure constraints. (Ayesha Rascoe, "Analysis: Tapping oil from reserve may be trickier than ever," Reuters, March 16, 2012.)

[90] The rest is held by companies for commercial reasons or because they are mandated by their government to hold stocks at certain levels to meet IEA requirements. Most European IEA members meet much of their obligation by mandating that companies hold a certain level of refined product stocks in case of emergency. In contrast, the United States and IEA members in the Pacific meet most of their obligation through government-held crude stockpiles. The obligation does not apply to net exporting members such as Canada. Data from David Fyfe et al., *Oil Market Report (March, 2012)*, International Energy Agency, March 14, 2011, http://omrpublic.iea.org/omrarchive/14mar12full.pdf.

[91] International Energy Agency, *Fact Sheet: IEA Stocks and Drawdown Capacity*, February 25, 2011, http://www.iea.org/files/Potential_IEA_Stockdraw_Capacity.pdf.

of strategic stockpiles can help offset the impact of disruptions and may have contributed to oil prices being lower than they might have otherwise been.

The SPR provides a short term tool to respond to sudden supply disruptions at home or abroad. In 2012, the potential loss of Iranian exports to the market is not a physical disruption quite like the historic examples mentioned above. Nonetheless, tightening U.S. and EU sanctions policy appears to be having a similar effect by making Iranian crude more difficult to sell and potentially keeping some of it off the market.[92] Correspondingly, former purchasers of Iranian crude oil are looking for supply elsewhere, potentially bidding up global oil prices, including those faced by U.S. consumers. Further, there are currently disruptions reducing supply from elsewhere, including Sudan, Syria, and Yemen. This has prompted some to argue for a release of the SPR to contribute to lower oil prices and reduce the burden of import costs on the U.S. economy.[93]

Foreign disruptions for which an SPR drawdown may be considered include disruptions to sources of U.S. imports or disruptions of sources the United States does not directly import from but which can affect the availability of global oil supply (and prices) as was largely the case in the release of crude in the Summer of 2011. But what constitutes a significant enough supply disruption is debated. On the one hand, releasing crude oil from the SPR leaves less oil to use in case there are future disruptions and leaves open the risk that the SPR may have to be refilled at higher prices in the future. Being too cautious about the use of the SPR, on the other hand, may mean its full value is never utilized. Further, market participants, including oil exporting countries, may discount the possibility that the United States would use this policy tool in the future. SPR issues are considered in greater detail in CRS Report R41687, *The Strategic Petroleum Reserve and Refined Product Reserves: Authorization and Drawdown Policy*, by Anthony Andrews and Robert Pirog.

---

[92] For more about Iran and the impact on oil prices, see CRS Report R42382, *Rising Gasoline Prices 2012*, by Neelesh Nerurkar and Robert Pirog.

[93] Philip K. Verleger, *Using US Strategic Reserves to Moderate Potential Oil Price Increases from Sanctions on Iran*, Peterson Institute for International Economics, February 2012, http://www.iie.com/publications/interstitial.cfm?ResearchID=2048.

Appendix. Petroleum Tariff Rates

Table A-1. Normal Petroleum Import Tariffs Under the Harmonized Tariff Schedule of the United States (HTSUS)

Petroleum Categories	Normal Tariff
Petroleum oils and oils from bituminous minerals, crude, testing 25 degrees API gravity or more.	10.5¢/bbl
Petroleum oils and oils from bituminous minerals, crude, testing under 25 degrees API gravity.	5.25¢/bbl
Naphthas (excluding motor fuel/motor fuel blend stock) from petroleum oils and bituminous minerals (other than crude) or preparations 70% plus by weight from petroleum oils.	10.5¢/bbl
Distillate and residual fuel oil (including blends) derived from petroleum or oils from bituminous minerals, testing under 25 degrees API gravity.	5.25¢/bbl
Light oil mixture of hydrocarbons from petroleum oils and bituminous minerals (other than crude) or preparations 70% plus by weight from petroleum oils, not otherwise specified, not over 50% any single hydrocarbon.	10.5¢/bbl
Light oil motor fuel from petroleum oils and bituminous minerals (other than crude) or preparations 70% plus by weight from petroleum oils.	52.5¢/bbl
Distillate and residual fuel oil (including blends) derived from petroleum oils or oil of bituminous minerals, testing 25 degree API gravity.	10.5¢/bbl
Lubricating oils, with or without additives from petroleum oils and bitumen minerals (other than crude) or preparations 70% plus by weight from petroleum oils.	84¢/bbl
Light oil motor fuel blending stock from petroleum oils and bituminous minerals (other than crude) or preparations 70% plus by weight from petroleum oils.	52.5¢/bbl

Source: Harmonized Tariff Schedule Chapter 27. Categories identified by the International Trade Administration.

Notes: "bbl" stands for barrel (42 gallons). API gravity is a measure for the specific gravity of oil developed by the American Petroleum Institute and others. The higher the number, the lighter and less dense the oil. Lighter oils tend to require less processing and yield more valuable products.

Author Contact Information

Neelesh Nerurkar
Specialist in Energy Policy
nnerurkar@crs.loc.gov, 7-2873

www.ingramcontent.com/pod-product-compliance
Lightning Source LLC
Chambersburg PA
CBHW081408170526

45166CB00010B/3257